Small Business Management

Editor:
Frank Dawes

BLACKHALL
Publishing

This book was typeset by Artwerk for

Blackhall Publishing
26 Eustace Street
Dublin 2
Ireland
e-mail: blackhall@tinet.ie

© Frank Dawes, 1999
individual contributors

ISBN: 1 901657 59 0

Printed in Ireland by
Betaprint Ltd.

Contents

7: LEADERSHIP AND STRATEGY CHALLENGES 139
David MacGregor

List of Figures

Chapter 1

Chapter 2

Chapter 3

List of Tables

List of Contributors

Frank Dawes, Director of the Centre for Enterprise and Management (CEM), Bolton Institute of Higher Education. *Research interests* – Management learning and development. The impact of managerial style on business performance in the small business sector.

Terry Elliott, Senior Lecturer in Financial Management and Accounting, CEM, Bolton Institute of Higher Education. *Research interests* – Financial management in the small firm.

Wes Haydock, Principal Lecturer in Management, CEM, Bolton Institute of Higher Education. *Research interests* – Human Resource Management, Management Development, Teamworking.

David MacGregor, Senior Lecturer in Strategic Management, Manchester Metropolitan University. *Research interests* – Strategic management in small firms, craft-based musical instrument manufacturers.

Dr Peter Moran, Senior Lecturer in Organisational Behaviour, CEM, Bolton Institute of Higher Education. *Research interests* – The organisation and management of the emergency services, failure proneness in business organisations, consultant interventions in SMEs.

Tony Scott, Senior Lecturer and computer consultant, CEM, Bolton Institute of Higher Education. *Research interests* – Rapid Application Development.

Tim Smith, Senior Lecturer in Marketing, CEM, Bolton Institute of Higher Education. *Research interests* – Market appraisal and entry strategies in small businesses.

Frank Sutton, PhD student, Bolton Business School, Bolton Institute of Higher Education. *Research interests* – Consultant interventions and failure proneness in SMEs.

Dedication

To those managers and directors of small businesses involved in the development of the MBA in Small Business Management.

Introduction

The origins of the book arose from the work carried out at Bolton Institute in developing and delivering the first UK-based MBA in Small Business Management. The need for a specialised MBA programme for small business came about for a number of reasons.

Firstly, managers from the small business sector who had embarked on the general MBA programme at Bolton often had difficulty in linking traditional theories from management texts to their own business environment.

Secondly, these managers not only wanted to develop their own skills and knowledge, but also wanted and needed to develop their organisation as well. The general MBA programme did not have the flexibility in structure and assessment to always allow this to take place.

Thirdly, research conducted in 1994 with a small group of directors from a range of small and medium-sized firms aimed to evaluate the relevance of competence-based standards for senior managers. These standards provided a focal point for identifying the areas of competence needed to guide the strategic development of businesses. What emerged from this research project was that these standards, which had been developed by the Management Charter Initiative, were of relevance to the small firms that had been engaged in the research project. However, there was a clear proviso linked to this general conclusion. The directors involved in the project stated that if they were to commit themselves and others to a management training and development programme, the provision needed to not only be relevant to the individual's personal needs but also to their organisation. The issue was that a development framework was needed that linked personal development with the job role set within the organisational context.

This research progressed when the Department of Education and Employment provided funding in 1995 for the development of an MBA focused on the needs of the small business sector. The programme is focused particularly on those established small firms that wish to develop and grow. The MBA in Small Business Management was launched in the autumn of 1996. It was aimed at managers in small and medium-sized firms who had been established for a number of years and who were looking to develop their business.

One of the aims of developing the MBA was to establish links with senior managers and decision-makers in the small business sector to engage them in the ongoing development of the programme and the discussion of emergent research findings. Some of the content within the book reflects contributions from those who have participated in the workshops and who have been involved in the research linked to the MBA. It is hoped that the material in the book accurately reflects many of the management challenges that are faced by small businesses.

A great deal of research has developed around small firms and the enterprise culture, with a growing body of literature supporting this work. There are, however, many gaps in the knowledge available on small firms and entrepreneurial behaviour. For example, the entrepreneurial characteristics linked with success have been the subject of much research, but little has focused on those characteristics linked to failure. Chapter 4 considers some of the overlooked issues.

Criticism surrounds the validity of some research carried out in small firms, specifically in relation to the general conclusions that can be drawn. An example of this is related to training in small and medium-sized firms and the link to subsequent enhanced performance. It has been recognised by a number of writers, including Gibb (1990; 1996) and Kirby (1990), that management training provided for the small business sector is often unsuitable and too particular. Gibb (1996) criticises the providers of this training for teaching in a "non-enterprising manner". He highlights the important aspect of an enterprising approach to management as the concentration on development processes and on how to solve problems. This issue of educating and developing managers from small businesses in an appropriate manner that meets their individual and business needs would seem to be an essential aspect of supporting the development of small firms. In addition to this, Gibb (1997) suggests that the education needs of small businesses must focus on the manager(s) as well as the learning needs of the stakeholders with whom they interact.

As the body of literature develops around the small business sector we can expect that many current views and assumptions will be challenged and new ones will emerge. Arising from the research carried out in developing the MBA in Small Business Management, a number of issues were identified that challenged the traditional business school approach to management development provision. It highlighted the need to reorientate the existing programme so that supply-side issues of environment, delivery mechanisms and the tradition of business education, which focuses on conceptual frameworks relevant only to large organisations, were addressed.

This book provides an introduction to the key challenges facing small businesses in their attempt to survive and grow. It aims to provide an insight into these challenges using small case studies to illustrate key issues and provide opportunities to learn from them.

It is intended that the book will be of interest to managers in small businesses who wish to develop their understanding of the potential challenges facing them. Business advisers and counsellors to small firms will also find the book of interest, as the case studies used are real scenarios that many of them will be able to relate to. Because the book uses an approach which highlights key challenges faced by small businesses, students wishing to develop an insight into this area will find that the small case studies allow them to gain access to the 'live' problems facing this sector.

Chapter 1 begins by considering the definition of what constitutes a small business and provides a discussion of the general problems they face, including the barriers to growth and inadequacies of the support provided by various agencies. The role of self-development as an approach to improving managerial skills is of relevance to small business managers as they adapt their education to reflect the challenges affecting their business within today's dynamic environment.

Chapter 2 provides a focal point for considering how management self-development can be used to direct individual learning needs. Not only is the development of the small firm manager important in the competitiveness of the firm, but the development of a team to build the business is vital as well.

Chapter 3 considers the criteria for building a successful team to develop the business and also focuses on the thorny subject of the need to utilise external experts for the development and implementation of information technology strategies. The chapter considers how the need to develop joint learning between the two sets of stakeholders in this situation is paramount to the successful development and implementation of these projects.

Chapter 4 examines the issue of business failure, which is often attributed to the lack of skills and knowledge within the small business without recognising that there are other factors, such as entrepreneurial personality, that are more difficult to identify. This chapter highlights a case study that examines the personality traits of an entrepreneur alongside the concept of business growth and the potential for failure.

Chapter 5 looks at the financial and non-financial performance factors that need to be identified in relation to the relevant competitive factors faced by individual small firms. It provides two case studies that examine the way in which two organisations have sought to overcome key problems brought about by a lack of appropriate operational monitoring and control.

Chapter 6 explores the need for small firms and their managers to develop an understanding of their competitive environment alongside the need to develop a marketing orientation in relation to business planning. Two case studies are used to illustrate the need for small businesses to become more marketing-oriented in relation to business planning.

Chapter 7 provides a fresh insight into the process of strategic management in the small business context. It highlights the difficulty in applying traditional approaches to strategic planning in the small business context.

References

Gibb, A A, "Training the Trainers for Small Business" *Journal of European Industrial Training* (1990) Vol. 14, No.1.

Gibb, A A, "Entrepreneurship and Small Business Management: Can we Afford to Neglect them in the 21st Century Business School?" *British Journal of Management* (1996) Vol. 7, No. 4, pp. 309-321.

Gibb, A A, "Small Firms' Training and Competitiveness: Building upon the Small Business as a Learning Organisation" *International Small Business Journal* (1997) Vol. 15, No. 3, pp. 13-30.

Kirby, D A, "Management Education and Small Business Development: An Exploratory Study of Small Firms in Business" *Journal of Small Business Management* (1990) Vol. 28, No. 4.

Chapter 1

DEFINING SMALL FIRMS AND THEIR KEY CHALLENGES

Frank Dawes and Wes Haydock

Introduction

The importance of the small and medium-sized enterprise (SME) sector to the UK economy has been well documented, and the problems encountered by these firms as they grow has been the focus of much attention, particularly in the 1980s and 1990s. One of the reasons for this has been a belief that a vibrant small business sector can make a significant impact on the local economy. Many small firms have limited ambitions for growth but provide an important source of employment in local communities and give independence and status to their owners. These types of firms give a sound economic base to many regions and towns.

It is also recognised that the flexibility, adaptiveness and responsiveness of small businesses allows them to react quickly to changes in the competitive environment. Small firms are also seen as a key source of innovation, providing new types of products and services and new ways of delivering old services. To some extent this has provided a model that many larger firms have adopted in restructuring their business in an attempt to get closer to customers.

Commentators draw attention to the role that small firms have played in the economies of Japan, Germany and the United States. In these economies as well as the UK the predominant employers are now small to medium-sized firms. DTI (1997) figures for the UK identify that small to medium-sized firms employ in excess of 60 per cent of the total workforce and produce over 60 per cent of the total turnover in the UK.

Defining the Small Business Sector

Precisely what is a small firm? Definitions vary depending on criteria such as number of employees and turnover. The 1971 Bolton Report took into consideration that in different industrial sectors, the number of employees might be an inappropriate indicator of size. It recommended that small firms be defined by various criteria, including numbers of employees (which varied across industrial sectors), turnover *and* an economic definition that was based on the essential characteristics of a small firm. These characteristics were that it:

• has a small share of the market;
• operates independently;
• is an 'owner-managed' organisation.

The difficulty of applying these differing and sometimes conflicting criteria has led many who have an interest in this sector to revert to the European Union (EU) definition of the small to medium-sized enterprise as a distinct entity employing less than 500 employees. The problem with this definition is that this covers 99 per cent of all firms in the UK.

A more precise definition of the different types of firms falling in this range is also offered by the EU:

Type of firm	Number of employees
Micro	1 - 9
Small	10 - 99
Medium	100 - 499

In the UK it is the micro-business that dominates, with over 94 per cent of all firms found in this sector, whilst less than 1 per cent fall within the medium-sized range. In Germany, this medium-sized range, the *Mittelsand* sector, has been identified as one of the key sources of their previous economic success. It has been suggested that the dominance of the micro-business sector in the UK could be a source of weakness because of the high failure rates associated with very small firms.

The emphasis on developing an enterprise culture has led policy makers throughout the 1980s and 1990s to focus on increasing the number of business start-ups as a means of providing measurable outcomes to initiatives. The sad fact is that many of these will not survive beyond the first year. Stanworth and Gray (1990) identified that the chances of a new firm employing 100 people within a decade are less than 1 per cent.

A regular monitor of the problems faced by small firms is provided by the NatWest/SBRT quarterly survey of small businesses in Britain. The main problems identified by respondents between 1997 and 1999 are:

- low turnover;
- government regulations and paperwork;
- lack of skilled/trained employees;
- cash flow/late payments.

This has led to researchers and policy makers seeking to identify small firms that have the potential and desire to grow.

Challenges to Small Firm Growth

The assumption that all small firms wish to grow is a fallacy. There are many people who start businesses where self-employment or a 'lifestyle' business is the primary aim. However, for those firms whose main aim is growth, there are a number of challenges that have to be faced.

For many owners of small firms the requirement to control matters inhibits them from bringing in outside shareholders to help expand and develop the business. The need to remain independent and maintain control of their future is central to many small business owners. Growing the business involves 'letting go' of certain activities, and Hendry *et al.* (1995) argues that it is a *team* that grows the business, not an individual. Timmons states "a substantial amount of research, as well as practical experience, confirms that a team grows a business while a solo entrepreneur makes a living".[1]

---

1. Timmons, JA, " New Venture Creation Entrepreneurship in the 1990s" in Hendry *et al.*, *Strategy Through People* (London: Routledge) 1995, pp.16-17.

Birley (1997) found that research conducted across seventeen countries in Europe concerning the relationship between growth and control produced findings that identified four quite separate business types. These are:

1. The *protectionists* who wanted to maintain their current business at its current size, thus protecting their investment.
2. The *business-orientated* who combined growth and control goals with a need to protect their income and their investment.
3. The *dynasts* who wanted to grow their business, protect their investment and pass it to the next generation.
4. The *family businesses* who wanted to keep their business at the current level and pass it on to the next generation.

Moran (1997) examines the mainstream approaches that have been used by a variety of people to study barriers to growth in the small business sector. He considers the barriers to growth brought about by the external business environment as well as the internal factors identified by Birley. He comments that:

> *...although practitioners operating in widely varying contexts may find one approach of more immediate use than others, there is the more subtle danger that in concentrating on one, the potential value of the others, which may not be immediately apparent, is lost.*[2]

Clearly, the range and diversity of small firms within the economy provides difficulty in developing a generic framework for analysing the barriers to growth.

Deakins (1996) points to a number of studies that suggest that the age of a firm is a significant aspect in determining growth rate, with younger firms achieving higher growth rates than older firms. The premise that the growth rate of a firm is linked to age is based on the view that all firms will go through several distinct stages of growth. The concept of the organisational life cycle has provided the focus for several models to be developed by authors such as Steinmetz (1969), Greiner (1972) and Churchill and Lewis (1983).

---

2. Moran, P, "Barriers to Growth in the SME Sector" *Enterprise and Growth in the Small Firm Sector* (Bolton: Bolton Business School Press) 1997, p. 9.

In 1994 Churchill re-examined the five-stage model from 1983 and extended it to six stages. Each stage of the model is characterised by what Churchill describes as "an index of increasing size, complexity and or dispersion".[3] He uses five management factors:

- managerial style;
- organisational structure;
- extent of formal systems;
- major strategic goals;
- the involvement of the owner in the business.

The model outlined below allows owners to assess the type of challenges facing them at current and future stages.

1. Conception/Existence

At this stage the organisation is simple and straightforward: the owner does everything. They are the driving force, seeking out new customers, developing new products or services, dealing with orders, managing cash flow and responding to faxes. The sole aim of the business at this stage is to survive – they will typically be looking to expand their customer base and gain enough cash to cover the demands of starting up a business.

Business systems to manage cash will be simple and any formal planning will probably be non-existent. Many firms never gain enough business to remain viable and the owners may have to close the business.

2. Survival

Firms that stay in business beyond stage one have demonstrated that they are a viable business. There will be a simple management structure in place, but they will have limited decision-making powers – the owner will make all significant decisions. The major goal for the firm is survival and to this end there is likely to be limited formal planning in the form of cash projections.

---

3. Churchill, N C, "The Six Key Phases of Company Growth" in S Birley & D F Muzyka (eds), *Mastering Enterprise*, (London: Financial Times/Pitman Publishing 1997).

The survival of the business will still be largely in the hands of the owner. Many businesses will remain at this stage for a long time and are typically restricted by growth opportunities in an overcrowded market sector or by the lack of ambition of the owner. Those businesses that become profitable will move on to the next stage and a fresh set of challenges.

3. Profitability and stabilisation

At this stage, the owner of the firm has recognised that they require further management skills to sustain profits and there will be a management team in place with key skills in areas such as finance and in planning and scheduling work activities. Basic systems will have been developed to monitor and manage finance and key operations. The structure of the firm will have developed along functional lines with the owner delegating some areas of responsibility for operational issues.

Due to market size and the niche that many small firms operate in many companies stay for long periods in the stability phase, providing the firm can adapt to external environmental changes. If it cannot adapt to these changes it will either fail or drop back to the survival stage.

4. Profitability and growth

In order to move successfully through to this stage, the firm will need to be able to not only identify opportunities but also put in place the resources necessary to meet these opportunities. One of the key resources will be finance – the cash and borrowing power of the firm will need to be put at risk to finance this growth and grasp the opportunities identified. In addition to this the managerial skills required within the team will need to be enhanced. Strategic planning will need to be developed jointly by the owner and the key managers so that they understand and are committed to the growth targets and appreciate the managerial challenges facing the firm. Operational planning will need to be delegated but the owner remains active in all aspects of the company's affairs.

Systems will need to be improved so that a larger and often more diverse organisation can be managed adequately. Stage four is often a first attempt to expand beyond its local roots; if the company is unsuccessful it may be possible to shift back to stage three or stage two, providing the cause(s) are detected in time. Success at this stage can allow the firm to commit itself to further growth into stage five.

5. Take-off

At this point the successful business may decide to consolidate and expand, moving from a regional expansion in stage four to a business with potential national and international coverage in stage five.

This brings with it a series of challenges which must be overcome in relation to achieving and financing rapid growth. The most important problems are in relation to delegation, the management of cash to fund growth and the control of costs. Key issues related to this are the:

- competence of the management team;
- skills of key people;
- style of management – the ability of the owner (if they are still there) to delegate further responsibilities;
- structure of the business in order to deal effectively with a more complex operating environment;
- ability to fund growth from the cash in the business and/or securing additional sources of finance;
- refinement of business systems which have become strained by the growth – the strategic planning systems that need to become more formalised in order to establish clear objectives for the business.

Very often firms that move successfully through the first four stages fail to succeed at stage five because of their inability to deal with the challenges outlined above. In these cases retrenchment can be achieved, although complete failure can ensue.

6. Maturity

Firms that move into this stage need to be aware of the dangers it can bring – failure to remain flexible and responsive to marke'

changes can ultimately result in decline. In the mature stage, a firm
will have established sound management and clear systems to control the business. The challenge, however, is to remain competitive
by not stifling creativity and innovation within planning systems
which fail to recognise changing environmental trends.

Figure 1 summarises the key challenges facing the small firm
in its quest for growth.

Figure 1: The key challenges facing the growing small firm

Stage of Growth	Key Challenges
1. Conception/ Existence	1. Expansion of customer base and increase in turnover. 2. Managing cash flow.
2. Survival	1. Improving the quality of products or services to consistently meet customers' increasing needs. 2. Generating sufficient revenue to remain profitable and replace capital equipment. 3. Developing the owner's manage ment skills and establishing a 'team' of key personnel in areas such as sales.
3. Profitability and stabilisation	1. Putting a management team in place to manage key functional areas. 2. Developing business systems to assist operational planning and financial control. 3. The ability to delegate – the owner 'letting go' of certain operational areas of responsibility.

4. Profitability and growth	1. Generating sufficient cash to develop the business. 2. Improving the managerial skills of the team so that growth can be managed successfully. 3. Improving the skills of people throughout the business. 4. Developing and implementing a clear approach to strategic planning.
5. Take-off	1. Delegating responsibility for operational control within a divisionalised structure. 2. Management know-how to manage a complex business. 3. Putting new or refined systems in place to manage a more complex business.
6. Maturity	1. Retaining the key factors that have brought about competitive success, such as flexibility of response and innovation in decision-making. 2. Identifying and responding to changes in the environment before competitors do.

The key point to emerge from this discussion is that there is a clear relationship between the levels of management expertise, business systems, team development, individual skills and the successful growth of the small firm.

Management skills and competence in areas such as developing strategic vision, communication, gaining commitment and managing performance are vital – firms that rate low in these areas are unlikely to meet the challenges of growth.

It also has to be recognised that the managerial challenges shift in emphasis as the business moves through the stages of growth. In the early stages, the success (or survival) of the company is directly related to the owner's abilities and talents. This factor is of prime importance. As the company develops and grows, a management team with specialised skills is required to support and then supplant the owner's skills. The manager needs to develop a broader range of management skills and spend more time managing the business through the team. The inability of many entrepreneurs to 'let go' and manage the growth of the business through their team explains why so many businesses fail to reach stage four (profitability and growth).

Learning as a Component in Small Firm Competitiveness

Support for small firms in the form of initiatives from the government to help them learn and improve their competitiveness has been varied. Underpinning many of these has been a common agreement that a well-trained workforce is a key factor in the performance of individual firms. In a review of studies that explored the impact of training initiatives on small firm performance, Westhead and Storey (1997) identified that there was an absence of any statistical evidence which proves that there is a causal link between small firm training provision and enhanced business performance. They suggest that more studies are needed to investigate the impact of training on small firms over periods greater than three years.

A particular aspect of training, that of updating managerial skills and knowledge within a small firm, has been recognised as a significant challenge that needs to be dealt with in a successful manner if a firm is to grow. Understanding and developing a learning environment that is appropriate for managers in small firms is a challenge that has often been missed by providers of management training and education.

Over the years a limiting factor in the development of small business managers in the UK has been the lack of suitable management programmes. Kirby (1990) identified that the majority of management development undertaken in the small firm sector was unstructured and too particular. This was supported by Gibb (1990), who suggested that conventional approaches to management training were inadequate to meet the needs of the small business sector. In a subsequent article Gibb (1996) identified the key aspects that needed to be incorporated into an 'enterprising' approach to teaching managers from small firms. Research carried out at Bolton Business School in developing an MBA in Small Business Management identified that the programme needed to:

- be flexible so that workshops can be responsive to managers' needs;
- limit time away from the workplace;
- integrate individual, team and business development;
- negotiate learning outcomes so that they meet the needs of the job, the person and their firm;
- allow managers to have ownership of their learning;
- utilise the workplace as part of the learning environment.

In the context of the small firm, the manager needs to not only learn new skills and knowledge but also adapt their behaviour in order to effectively apply these skills.

The programme was designed to examine issues of growth and focus managers on problematic areas affecting their organisations; the workshops therefore vary in emphasis between different groups on the programme. Company visits are used to negotiate learning objectives, allowing the work to be linked to individual and organisational requirements. A critical reflection and evaluation is built into each piece of work, allowing individual managers to assess the impact of the learning process on themselves and their organisation. Figure 2 below provides a contrast between the traditional approach to teaching, Gibb's enterprising approach and the one developed at Bolton for the MBA in Small Business Management.

Figure 2: Approaches to teaching

Traditional Approach	Bolton Approach	Enterprising Approach
Major focus on content.	Uses content to stimulate conceptualisation of issues.	Major focus on process.
Tutor led and dominated.	Tutor supported but with input.	Learner owns process.
Emphasis on 'know what'.	Emphasis on 'know why'.	Emphasis on 'know how'
Sessions heavily programmed.	Sessions structured but flexible.	Sessions flexible but responsive.
Learning objectives imposed.	Learning objectives negotiated but bounded.	Learning objectives negotiated.
Mistakes frowned upon.	Learn from others' mistakes through case study analysis. Reconciles theory and practice.	Learn from mistakes.
Emphasis on theory. Subject/functional focus.	Strategic focus.	Learn from practice. Multidisciplinary focus.

Source: D MacGregor, Bolton Business School

An important factor in this learning process is the starting point. Traditional approaches often start from what the teacher knows rather than what the learner already has experienced. Gibb (1997) suggests that 'traditional' approaches have less impact on the small firm manager because they fail to help managers identify and use knowledge gained from experience.

The Learning Cycle

The four-stage cyclical model of experiential learning developed by David Kolb (1984) acknowledges the importance of an individual's experience within the learning process. Individuals' actions lead to *concrete experiences (CE)* which provide us with a basis for reflection; *reflective observation (RO)* takes place when we stand back and think about our experiences and analyse the outcomes of these. This leads to the development of ideas about how things relate to one another – Kolb refers to this as *abstract conceptualisation (AC)*. Following this stage of the cycle, ideas are put into practice to see if they lead to improvements. This *active experimentation (AE)* stage leads to new experiences, which feeds again into the learning cycle. Figure 3 below illustrates this.

David Kolb's model of 'the learning cycle' identifies a four-stage process of the way that people learn. According to Kolb, for learners to be effective they need to use all four learning approaches. They need to "be able to involve themselves fully, openly, and without bias in new experiences (CE); reflect on and observe these experiences from many perspectives (RO); create concepts that integrate their observations into logically sound theories (AC); and use these theories to make decisions and solve problems (AE)" (Kolb, 1996: 273). A person who fails to use any one of the four approaches is likely to miss opportunities for learning.

An extreme example might be the type of person who only learns from experiences. This person is likely to say, "if I haven't seen it then it can't be true". This person can be contrasted to one who believes what they read but doesn't actually seek concrete experiences. In the academic world we call these people "bookworms". Although becoming highly skilled in all four approaches is desirable, there are problems in achieving this, the main one being that the "learning requires abilities that are polar opposites" and that "the learner, as a result, must continually choose which set of learning abilities to bring to bear in any particular situation".[4]

A simplified version of Kolb's model appears below:

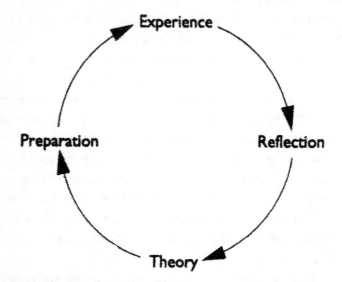

Kolb's work was modified by Peter Honey and Alan Mumford (1980), who "produced a questionnaire with twenty questions aimed at each of the four learning preferences so that students can find their preferred learning style. Cotton claims that the "most intelligent" adult learners come out with a very evenly balanced profile between the four styles. This would point to a "general observation that effective learners use all four approaches".[5]

Case studies A and B provide examples of managers who have used the concepts of the learning style theory to develop their managerial skills and approaches.

Case Study A

Mark is an owner-manager of a small advertising and marketing company employing ten staff. Mark described himself as a very practical person who likes to get stuck in and do things. "I don't like wasting time holding meetings and pro-

---

4. Kolb, D, "Management and the Learning Process" in K Starkey (ed)., *How Organisation Learn* (London: Thompson Business Press) 1996, p.273.
5. Cotton, L, *The Theory of Learners* (London: Kogan Page) 1995, p.133.

liferating," he stated. Mark's business was relatively successful but he felt that there were changes going on in the
industry that he had not caught up with. "I've seen what
some of our competitors can do and it's pretty impressive,"
he explained. "So far we've not lost orders because we excel
at delivering high quality goods on time to our regular customers." Mark realised that the technology he was using
was losing its competitive edge. His competitors were using
the latest technology and they could now produce material
that Mark's company could not.

Mark's learning style profile identified him as a 'reflec-
tor' and 'activist'. He scored very low on 'theorist' and fairly low on 'pragmatist'. Mark liked to involve himself fully in
new experiences and then to stand back and ponder. The
problem was that he did not look externally for new concepts
and theories, so he tended to get stuck in the day to day
issues. His high regard for reflecting resulted in many unan-
swered questions, and Mark was unable to focus on a few
ideas and bring them together into a concrete action plan.
Mark then attempted to develop his ability to 'theorise' and
'plan'. He made a specific point of drawing up an action
plan at the end of every meeting. Sometimes this meant that
implementation was left to someone else. In addition, he
contacted some equipment suppliers and organised visits to
get to understand what developments were occurring in this
field. He involved some of his staff in this.

Mark may not have needed the learning style profile to change the
way he managed. It did, however, act as a catalyst. Sharing his
concerns and issues with his staff also proved to be beneficial in
that this has led to increased understanding. The next case study
involves a young graduate who, in contrast to Mark, hardly
reflects at all.

Case Study B
Peter Yates is the Deputy General Manager at a transport
distribution company. He is a 27-year-old graduate and has

been employed by the company for four years. Peter's career prospects at the company appeared to be fading when his immediate boss, Graham, expressed concern with his performance at an annual appraisal interview. Peter was astonished since nothing had been mentioned to him before. However, Peter had realised that his manager seemed better able to cope with changing circumstances and situations than he did. Graham commented, "You come up with all these different ideas and proposals and we support you and implement them but then you shift to something else – why can't you just sort out one thing at a time?" Peter argued that once the change was made he didn't think it was anything to do with him anymore. "That's not really the point," stated Graham, "the problem is that you simply don't reflect on what you do – you're like a slippery eel."

Peter was advised to look at his personal approaches to work and came across learning style theory. He completed the Honey and Mumford inventory and the results were extremely revealing. His preference for 'doing' compared with 'reflecting' was remarkable. He hardly registered a score for 'reflecting' at all. "I know I was rather like that," he explained, "but I didn't know it was so extreme." Graham agreed to help Mark develop his reflecting abilities and they built this activity into their daily work. Mark was given the job of systematically reviewing actions taken before moving off to something else.

It must be emphasised that there is a danger of 'throwing the baby out with the bath water". Peter has a great aptitude for 'activism' and this should still be encouraged. What is important is that opportunities for learning and developing are not missed because of an over-concentration on one particular approach.

Whilst the learning cycle model is useful it is limited, as the single-loop nature of the model fails to include the formal acquisition of new skills and knowledge. This is important when considering the learning approach needed to improve business performance in small firms: management training and development programmes need to focus on the application of newly acquired management knowledge and skills to problems facing an organisation. The success of these programmes needs to be judged by the improvement in organisational practice.

To achieve this, a double-loop learning framework is needed that explicitly acknowledges the benefits of introducing new management skills and knowledge to the experiential learning cycle. The process of integrating new *management knowledge and skills* into the *reflective* element of the learning cycle allows an individual to review their *experiences* within the context of newly acquired knowledge and skills. This allows the manager to carry out an *evaluation of organisation practice* and develop new approaches to the situation under consideration, identifying areas for improvement. Testing these out takes place within the *experimentation* phase, which leads to new experiences.

Concurrent with this is the development of a deeper understanding of the relevance of theory and skills in real life situations. This Situational Learning Cycle shown in Figure 3 enables the individual manager to develop their *understanding of theory applied in practice,* which in turn provides the foundation for developing and acquiring *new knowledge and skills.*

Figure 3: Situational Learning Cycle

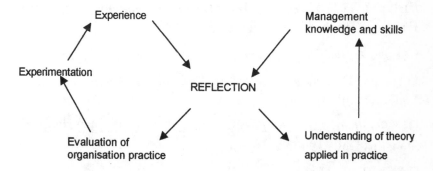

The situational learning cycle provides us with a framework within which collective learning can take place. Teams within a small firm can jointly participate in this approach to learning. Indeed, this team approach to learning has been highlighted by Dixon (1994) as an essential element for organisational learning to occur. Gibb (1997) has identified the concept of 'action-learning' developed by Revans (1985) as an essential concept if small firms are to learn better from their experience. Gibb also recognises that the small firm needs to learn from its key stakeholders if it is to survive.

Conclusion

The implications emerging from this first chapter are:
- small to medium-sized firms are a very important factor in the economy;
- the sector in the UK is dominated by micro-businesses;
- small firms face many barriers to growth that may cause failure;
- improving the capability of small firms to learn more effectively from their experiences is an essential aspect of improving competitiveness.

References

Birley, S, "To Grow or not to Grow" in S Birley & D F Muzyka (eds), *Mastering Enterprise* (London: Financial Times/Pitman Publishing) 1997.

Churchill, N C & V L Lewis, "The Five Stages of Business Growth" *Harvard Business Review* (1983) Vol. 61, No. 3, pp. 30-50.

Churchill, N C, "The Six Key Phases of Company Growth" in S Birley & D F Muzyka (eds), *Mastering Enterprise* (London Financial Times/ Pitman Publishing) 1997.

Cotton, V, *The Theory of Learners* (London: Kogan Page) 1995.

Deakins, D, *Entrepreneurship and Small Firms* (London: McGraw Hill) 1996.

DTI *Small Firms in the Economy* Statistical Bulletin (DTI SME Statistics Unit) 1997.

Greiner, L E, "Evolution and Revolution as Organisations Grow" *Harvard Business Review* (1972) Vol. 50, No. 4, pp. 37-46.

Gibb, A A, "Training the Trainers for Small Business" *Journal of European Industrial Training* (1990) Vol. 14, No.1.

Gibb, A A, "Entrepreneurship and Small Business Management: Can We Afford to Neglect Them in the 21st Century Business School?" *British Journal of Management* (1996) Vol. 7, No. 4, pp. 309-321.

Gibb, A A, "Small Firms' Training and Competitiveness: Building upon the Small Business as a Learning Organisation" *International Small Business Journal* (1997) Vol. 15, No. 3, pp. 13-30.

Hendry, *et al., Strategy Through People* (London: Routledge) 1995.

Kirby, D A, "Management Education and Small Business Development: An Exploratory Study of Small Firms in Business" *Journal of Small Business Management* (1990) Vol. 28, No. 4.

Kolb, D, *Experiential Learning* (New Jersey: Prentice Hall) 1984.

Kolb, D, "Management and the Learning Process" in K Starkey (ed.), *How Organisations Learn* (London: Thompson Business Press) 1996.

Moran, P, "Barriers to Growth in the SME Sector" in F Dawes *Enterprise and Growth in the Small Firm Sector* (Bolton: Bolton Business School Press) 1997.

NatWest/SBRT, *Natwest Quarterly Survey of Small Business in Britain* (London: Natwest/Small Business Research Trust) 1997-1999.

Stanworth, J & C Gray, "New Venture Creation Entrepreneurship in the 1990s" in Hendry *et al., Strategy Through People* (London: Routledge) 1995.

Steinmatz, I, "Critical Stages of Small Business Growth" *Business Horizons* (February 1969) pp. 29-36.

Timmons, J A, "New Venture Creation Entrepreneurship in the 1990s" in Hendry *et al., Strategy Through People* London: Routledge) 1995.

Westhead, P & D J Storey, "Training Provision and the Development of Small and Medium-Sized Enterprises" (Sudbury: DfEE Research Report No. 26) 1997.

Chapter 2

DEVELOPING MANAGERIAL SKILLS AND COMPETENCE

Wes Haydock

Introduction

The challenges facing modern businesses have resulted in the management process becoming increasingly complex. The fierce competitive pressures for price, quality and service "requires managers with the ability to grasp the key features in complex situations, and to think constructively and creatively about appropriate responses to these".[1] Much of the current literature on management adopts a contingency approach where "different problems and situations require different solutions".[2] Charles Handy has extended this dilemma through his provocative phase, "we used to think we knew how to manage businesses but now we know better" (Handy, 1992). The attempt to find simple solutions for all problems appears to be futile.

Despite the evidence that simple universal approaches to management do not work there is still much recent literature that attempts to find the 'right' way to manage. Managers who face increasing personal demands are attracted to these 'quick fix' remedies. In the 1980s, for example, Tom Peters' lectures attracted many managers who were prepared to pay hundreds of pounds just to hear his views about how a company can become 'excellent'. Rosebeth Moss Cantor had similar success with her lectures on creativity in organisations. Since then there has been no let up of 'airport' books that claim to reveal the secret of management and managing. These books are extremely popular. Managers are caught up in this search for the 'solution', but in

---

1. Pearce, S & S Cameron, *Against the Grain* (Oxford: Butterworth Heinemann) 1977, p. 13.
2. Hannagan, *Management Concepts and Practices* (London: Pitmann) 1998, p.16.

reality few believe that one exists. Why these books are so successful is something of a mystery. Is it that many managers continue this search because they feel that they have to do something? Sometimes managers do latch on to an idea but quickly
discard it and take up something else. This is usually referred to
as the 'flavour of the month' scenario. The adoption of fads
which are soon disregarded and replaced by something else usually confuses the workforce, which then becomes cynical.

If there are no simple quick fix solutions to the management
problem, what should managers do to improve the way they
manage? One answer lies in the management self-development
approach. Management self-development covers a wide range of
concepts that all require the manager to take responsibility for
his or her own learning and development. Under self-development, the manager must want to learn new skills and approaches.
This often flies in the face of our natural tendency to rely on our
current strengths. For example, there are parallels in sports and
music. In tennis we might strive to improve our second serve or
our backhand. Few of us would say, "my backhand is perfectly
okay". In music, the real challenges have occurred in the more
'progressive' areas. Sun Ra, the late avant-composer and big
band leader, once said, "there's no point in playing what you
know, what you want to do is to play what you don't know"
(Radio 3 broadcast, 1998). The challenge for managers is to
develop themselves in areas "that they don't know". In the context of this chapter, this development will be referred to as 'management self-development'.

Management Self-Development

Mike Pedlar and his colleagues defined self-development as
"personal development, with the manager taking primary
responsibility for her or his own learning and for choosing the
means to do this".[3] The process involves the managers reflect-

---

3. Pedlar, M J Burgoyne & T Boydell, *A Manager's Guide to Self-Development*
(London: McGraw Hill) 1986, p. 4.

ing on their experiences, assessing their strengths and weakness and analysing their preferences and style (Pedlar *et al.*, 1988). The manager then creates a plan to improve or develop him or herself in some way. On courses where this approach is used managers engage in a "learning contract" (Boak, 1991).

There are numerous devices that managers can use to analyse their preferred ways of working and their strengths and weaknesses. These include the ways that they relate to others, organise themselves, solve problems, negotiate, handle conflict and learn and assert themselves. By systematically evaluating themselves and by seeking feedback from others managers, they can achieve greater self-understanding and identify areas for improvement. This need for self-understanding was emphasized by Chris Bones, who writes, "it is only if you can appreciate your own skills base and the gaps there may be in it against your current role requirements that you can even begin to consider taking charge of your own development".[4] Bones strongly advocated a similar approach for all employees: "It is also true of those who work for you. If you can get them to own their personal development needs, the action you can develop jointly will be twice as powerful in addressing those needs, and, eventually, improving performance."

Another benefit that results from a manager gaining a greater self-awareness is that it helps managers understand others. The starting point for successful management self-development is the desire on the manager's part to develop and the existence of acceptable diagnostic devices.

Self-development is certainly not a 'quick fix' remedy but one that should be continuous. There are numerous ideas and theories that can assist in the self-development process. In this chapter the focus will be on 'personal competence' (using the Management Charter Initiative model), 'leadership'(Adair), and 'work preferences and team roles' (Margerison and McCann). The following sections will explain how managers can develop

---

4. Bones, Chris *The Self-Reliant Manager* (London: Routledge) 1994, p. 31.

themselves in their work roles using these theories and models. Real life case studies will be used to demonstrate practical application. Theoretical explanations will be provided but will be kept to a minimum.

Personal Competence

There is much confusion in the literature regarding the meaning of the terms 'competence' and 'competency'. The terms competency, its plural competencies, and competence are frequently used interchangeably. Klemp (1980) defined a *competency* as an underlying characteristic of a person that results in effective and/or superior performance in a job. *Competence*, on the other hand, refers to the outputs of behaviour. Therefore, a *competency* is what someone has and a *competence* refers to what they do. The National Vocational Qualifications (NVQs) in Management, which emerged in the UK in the early-1990s, attempted to define the competences that underpin effective management. These were separated into functional and personal competences (NFMED 1990). The functional competences described the functions of management, such as managing people, information, finance and operations, whilst the personal competences were more concerned with effectiveness and style. The Personal Competence Model (PCM) is comprised four of 'clusters' of competence and thirteen dimensions, as shown in Table 1.

Table 1: MCI personal competence model

Clusters of Competence	Dimensions of Competence
1. Planning to optimise the achievement of results.	1.1 Showing concern for excellence. 1.2 Setting and prioritising objectives. 1.3 Monitoring and responding to actual against planned activities.
2. Managing others to optimise results.	2.1 Showing sensitivity to the needs of others. 2.2 Relating to others. 2.3 Presenting oneself positively to others.
3. Managing oneself to optimise results.	3.1 Showing self-confidence and personal drive. 3.2 Managing personal emotions and stress. 3.3 Managing personal learning and development.
4. Using intellect to optimise results.	4.1 Collecting and organising information. 4.2 Identifying and applying concepts. 4.3 Making decisions.

NB: This Personal Competence Model appeared with the original NVQ competences. It has now been replaced with the publication of new standards.

There have been numerous other attempts to identify the personal competences required for effective management (see Pedlar,

Burgoyne & Boydell, 1978; Woodcock & Francis, 1996). The MCI standards (NFMED, 1990) also provide specific "behavioural indicators" that accompany each dimension of competence. The behavioural indicators for Dimension 2.1, "showing sensitivity to the needs of others" include, for example:

- "making time to be available to support others";

- "reinforce others' self-worth and value in what they do";

- "encourage others to express themselves honestly";

- "actively seek to identify and clarify the attitudes, views and feelings of others".

Managers can reflect on how well they perform these behavioural indicators through self-assessment and through the use of "upward/360 degree" techniques. "Upward/360 degree" appraisal has been advocated by many researchers (for example see Grint, 1993; Fletcher, 1996) and it is used by a number of organisations, including United Distillers and British Airways. This form of appraisal does not necessarily solve the problems associated with traditional "downward" appraisal. An employee appraising their manager, for example, faces the same problems regarding subjectivity as encountered in downward appraisal. What is gained by "Upward/360 degree" appraisal is a wider set of views. The greater perspective can provide the manager with richer feedback. A good example of upward appraisal involves John Egan, who was then General Manager of United Distillers. In his upward appraisal, every one of his senior managers said that he did not listen effectively to them. This was a surprise to John, who felt that he was a good listener. Receiving this type of feedback can, of course, be extremely threatening and embarrassing. Obtaining meaningful feedback from others should not be entered into lightly. If you do not want feedback then this process is not for you.

If self-assessment and upward feedback processes are acceptable to managers, then specifically designed questionnaires are available to facilitate this process. Connor and Haydock (1992) compiled two questionnaires, which they called "Personal Competence Inventories" (PCIs) to assist managers in identifying their competences against the MCI model. One inventory was for the manager's self-assessment and the other was a modified "360 degree" feedback version for the manager's colleagues to complete. The latter version could be given to anyone who had some knowledge of the manager's behaviour at work. This might include their immediate superior, their colleagues, those who report to them and even clients and customers. In this way, managers could evaluate their strengths and weaknesses and compare this with others' views about them.

The inventories are comprised of a number of questions based on the behavioural indicators. The managers have to state whether they always, often, sometimes, rarely or never demonstrated this behaviour. Interpreting the results of the questionnaires does not require an 'expert', so the manager can do this herself. It is, however, often useful to be able to talk through the findings with a colleague or 'mentor'. If confidentiality is a problem then it might be a good idea for a third party to compile the results.

The following two case studies involve managers who used the personal competence model and inventory in different ways.

Case Study A

Frank is a Financial Manager at Bollis, a chemical company employing approximately 200 staff. Frank issued the questionnaire to four other people, his immediate superior and to three people who reported to him. He emphasised that this was a developmental activity and that he wanted them to 'tell the truth'. Frank's scores were very similar to those recorded by his immediate boss. His scores were also similar to those of his staff with the exception of two dimensions in cluster 2. These were 'showing sensitivity to the needs of others' and 'relating to others'. In these two dimensions Frank scored himself better than his staff did. Frank did not understand why there was a discrepancy and his initial reaction was to circulate the questionnaire to more people so that he could find staff who agreed with his views.

Frank discussed the findings with a colleague, Jim, who acted as a 'mentor'. They studied the questions and the different responses. They also discussed why there might be such a difference. Frank reluctantly took up Jim's suggestion that he talk to the people who filled in the inventory. What emerged was that the staff had a different view regarding what they wanted from Frank. They felt that he was too detached, that he did not give them sufficient praise and that he did not encourage them to put forward suggestions and proposals. Frank admitted that this was his style. "I feel that as a manager I should keep some distance," he said. Frank, who described himself as a 'perfectionist', added, "the sort of praise that I want is to keep my job." Frank agreed to try to be more approachable and to involve his staff more in planning and decision making. Several months later there had been some improvement and the staff felt better about their jobs.

The process described above can only be successfully completed if the manager genuinely wants to receive feedback and improve the way he or she manages. Furthermore, many changes in the manager's behaviour will occur gradually, and there is the additional problem of the manager returning to previous behaviour in times of extra pressure. Any form of "upward/360 degree" appraisal is potentially problematic. There are ethical issues regarding, for example, whether those giving feedback should be anonymous. Given that Frank only had a few staff reporting directly to him, it was extremely difficult to provide anonymity. In case study two the situation was very different.

Case Study B

Alan also works for Bollis and is currently the Managing Director of one of the divisions. Alan adopted the same process as Frank, but in his case there were no obvious differences between his views about his personal competence and the views that others held. Alan scored well on most of the areas of competence with the exception of cluster 1. Alan and his colleagues were fairly critical of his

> *ability in "planning to optimise the achievement of results". The specific dimensions of competence that seemed to be the main problem were "setting and prioritising objectives" and "monitoring and responding to actual against planned activities". It turned out that the two dimensions of competence were related in that the absence of proper objectives resulted in the failure to monitor and respond. After discussing these issues with his colleagues, Alan realised that the problem was not so much to do with a failure to set objectives, but was that the objectives being set were too vague. As a result, Alan found a short training course on objective setting and this enabled him to set more specific objectives in the future.*

The two case studies above demonstrate how managers can develop their personal skills by reflecting on their skills and by seeking feedback from others. Anyone reading this book who would like to use the Personal Competence Inventories discussed in these case studies can get copies by writing to the author (see notes at end of this chapter for the address).

Leadership

There have been numerous attempts to identify the skills leaders should possess and what actions they should take (for example Reddin, 1987; Tannenbaum & Schmidt, 1957; Mintzberg, 1989; Blake & Mouton, 1964). Blake and Mouton's "managerial grid" comprises two axes that they labelled "concern for task" and "concern for people". John Adair (1984) developed this work and identified three needs that leaders must satisfy. These are "task needs", "group needs" and "individual needs". *Task needs* are those required to get the job done, *group needs* build and maintain teamworking and team spirit, and *individual needs* are those necessary for individuals to fulfil their personal goals, such as self-esteem and belonging.

According to Adair, the effectiveness of a leader depends on meeting the three overlapping needs within a work group. These

are the need to achieve a common task, the need for team maintenance and the individual needs of group members. All three
are equally important and the successful manager is one who
takes actions to satisfy them all.

Adair's 'Action Centred Leadership' model involves leaders
taking three forms of action:

1. **Actions that help achieve the task**. This is a fairly easy area
   because it is relatively simple to understand what the central
   task actually is. Actions include setting objectives, ensuring
   that targets and goals are communicated through to all staff,
   setting performance measurement and ensuring that progress
   is monitored.

2. **Actions that develop and motivate individuals**. This can be
   difficult because individuals bring with them both physical
   and psychological needs. The former includes security, food
   and shelter. The latter, which is far more difficult to satisfy,
   includes recognition, a sense of doing something worthwhile,
   status and the relationships that people form with each other.
   Managers' actions in this area include coaching, ensuring that
   individuals know where they fit in, training, the development
   of individuals and one on one communications.

3. **Actions that build and develop teams**. This area is also
   problematic. Teams are vital to the success of most organisations, but they form their own unwritten rules and standards
   of behaviour. The manager can influence successful teams
   through group maintenance activities, teambuilding, placing
   emphasis on teams to develop solutions to problems, helping
   individuals to understand others, resolving conflicts between
   members and by generally bringing the team together.

According to Adair, leaders should focus equally on each of the
three areas. Concentrating on just one or two areas has extreme
dangers since all three are essential for effective organisation.
For example, a manager who focuses too much on tasks and

teams is unlikely to pay sufficient attention to the individual needs of the staff. In such situations, the needs of individuals are likely to be ignored, which may well lead to individual personal disillusionment.

Of course, actions taken by managers do not fit neatly into just one of the three areas. Indeed, there are many activities that a manager can carry out that achieve more than one of these three overall aims at the same time. Armstrong (1994) made this point when he wrote that in reality these needs are independent and best expressed as three overlapping circles.

Despite the interdependency of the three needs, Adair produced a leadership style questionnaire which attempted to isolate actions that lead to satisfying the different needs. The questions that attempted to determine the manager's concern for task, people and teams. Case studies C and D demonstrate how two managers have used this 'Action Centred Leadership' model to develop their skills.

Case Study C

Until recently Susan was the owner-manager of an accountancy firm employing five staff. This year she merged her company with a larger company. This change involved a change in location for her office and the adoption of new staff. Susan's new role was as a partner where she managed an office of nine staff. At the time the new office was set up, Susan took three of her old employees with her, inherited three from the new company and had to recruit an additional three new staff. The result was a new work group who had at least three different cultures and approaches. Susan soon realised that the new group was not a 'team'. In her previous company she built the team up gradually over several years. She had no experience of the current situation and did not know what to do.

Susan started to look at theoretical approaches to management and leadership and she came across the action centred leadership model. She assessed herself using the model and immediately realised that her high concern for task outstripped a concern for teams and individuals. Gradually Susan started to introduce new approaches. She organised briefing sessions to give out information and to seek ideas and feedback from the staff. At first she made little progress. "They did not seem to be interested," she complained, "but I stuck at it, then one of the new members approached me with a proposal outside of the meeting. I took great care to listen carefully and encourage her and the next time we had a staff meeting I raised the matter with the others. Suddenly they all joined in. I feel now that we have more of a team and, whilst there is not always agreement on issues, we always manage to find a way forward that we can all go along with."

The next case study provides an example of a manager who paid insufficient attention to motivating the individual members of staff. In this case the manager encountered a labour turnover problem.

Case Study D

Mary is a manager of a small computer training company employing twelve staff. There were three different types of staff: trainers, secretaries and sales personnel. The main problem facing Mary was that there was a large labour turnover of sales staff. Mary blamed this on the type of work, which mainly involved telesales. "It's a problem throughout the industry," she exclaimed. Mary also used the action centred leadership model and the results indicated that she had a high concern for task and teams but a low concern for individuals. Basically she tended to treat everyone the same. "I think it is important to be consistent," she explained. Mary decided, however, to attempt to use what she had learnt about her leadership style and focus more on individuals. She organised a 'welcome' programme for new recruits but initially ran it for existing staff who she then asked for comments. She tried to include key information about the company. She discovered that the existing staff had incomplete knowledge about the company and its affairs. A resultant discussion produced a company mission statement and an improved 'welcome' programme. Mary also asked her existing staff for ideas about what they would like to see changed. She discovered that the staff wanted her to be more understanding about their personal problems and to be more open and friendly. Mary was surprised that the staff wanted more responsibility in the way the office was managed and she then tried to provide this. Several months later Mary had not lost any more staff and she felt happier about leaving the office to concentrate on more strategic issues.

Work Preferences and the Team Management Profile

The work of Charles Margerison and Dick McCann (*Team Management Sytems*) is most useful in helping managers improve their performance at work. They set out to understand why some teams were more successful than others. Their research identified eight different types of work which occur in teams. The eight types of work are advising, innovating, promoting, developing, organising, producing, inspecting and maintaining. Margerison and McCann (1995) place these into what they refer to as the "Types of Work Model", as follows:

Figure 1: Margerison-McCann Types of Work Model

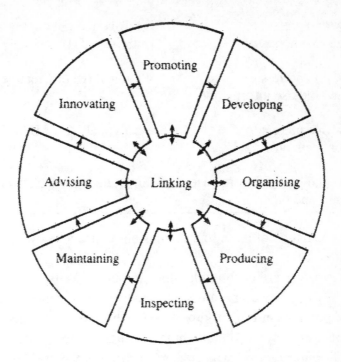

Reproduced with the kind permission of TMS Development International Ltd

Their research led them to conclude that people have preferences for carrying out different functions and that it is possible to measure a person's 'work preferences', which predicts the type of functions that person likes to perform. Margerison and McCann developed an instrument they named the "Team Management Profile Questionnaire", which is based on the following four dimensions:

Dimension	Work Preference
How one prefers to relate to others.	Extroverted (E) or Introverted (I)
How one prefers to gather and use information.	Practical (P) or Creative (C).
How one prefers to make decisions.	Analytical (A) or Belief (B).
How one prefers to organise oneself and others.	Structured (S) or Flexible (F).

An explanation of these four dimensions appears below.

- *Extroverts* prefer to think things through by talking out loud. They enjoy variety, are stimulated by interruptions, can be impulsive and are likely to contribute a lot at meetings. *Introverts* prefer to think things through before speaking, dislike interruptions, will prepare in depth when speaking publicly, tend to be quiet at meetings and are more likely to consider things before acting.

- *People who respond to information creatively* enjoy ambiguity, float new ideas, get bored with routine work, like complexity, often see the whole picture but miss out on detail and can have their 'head in the clouds'. *Those who prefer a practical approach* prefer clearly-defined problems, are down to earth, are patient with routine work, pay attention to facts and details, are often sound on details but may miss the whole picture.

- People who prefer to make decisions based on *analysis* try to establish objective decision-making criteria, measure decisions against payoffs, are open to change depending on the situation and negotiate the evidence. *Beliefs-oriented* people have personal/subjective decision-making criteria, measure decisions against beliefs and will resist change if it opposes their beliefs. They negotiate on the rights and wrongs of a situation, allow objectives to follow from beliefs, such as harmony based on common values, may become over-committed to a point of view and can be regarded as being stubborn.

- *Structured* people like clarity and order, develop and stick to plans, may rush to decisions with insufficient information, tend to keep to deadlines and dislike ambiguity, emphasise concluding and resolving rather than diagnosing. *Flexible* people may appear disorganised, are information orientated, will often change plans from day to day, are prone to information overload, are open-minded, tolerate ambiguity and emphasise diagnosing over concluding and resolving.

The "Team Management Profile Questionnaire" contains 60 questions that attempt to measure a person's work preferences in these four areas. The questions are relatively simple, but at the same time do not lead the person towards a particular answer. The scoring is simple to understand. The maximum score for any single preference is 30 and the minimum is zero. For example, a person may score 25 on the extrovert scale and 12 on the introvert scale. This tells us that this person is much more likely to demonstrate extroverted behaviour in their relationships. A person scoring 18 on the extrovert scale and 17 on the introvert one does not have a preference one way or the other. They are equally likely to portray extroverted or introverted behaviour, depending on the situation.

After completing the "Team Management Profile Questionnaire" managers obtain a "Team Management Profile", which includes their scores for the four dimensions together with an extremely thorough personal profile. These personal reports are the property of the individual concerned and they should only be shared with their colleagues with their permission. This is an ethical issue that Margerison and McCann insist on before anyone completes the questionnaire. Almost without exception managers express surprise and delight that they are able to see themselves accurately described in the report.

Figure 2: Margerison-McCann Team Management Wheel

Reproduced with the kind permission of TMS Development International Ltd

Margerison and McCann's theory is that the best teams are those that portray a range of work preferences, provided that the potential dysfunctionality of their differences could be managed. People with certain work preference combinations prefer to carry out particular functions. Certain functions, such as promoting, may be ignored or given low priority if there is an absence of people who prefer this activity. Whether this is a problem for the team depends largely on how important that activity is in achieving the overall task. Promoting may, for example, not be important. If promoting is important and there are no natural 'promoters' then this problem can be approached through either adding new members or through developing current team members. Sometimes it is sufficient for a team to say, "OK, let us all concentrate on promoting for a while because this is something that we do not do automatically".

People with opposite work preferences can be a perfect team providing they find ways of working together. Managers can assist work teams in this through developing what Margerison and McCann call 'linking skills'. This broadly relates to what others would call team management, or leadership skills. Linking skills involve co-ordinating and integrating the team-work functions and include problem solving and counselling, building team relationships, delegation, setting objectives, communication, setting standards and participative decision making. Two examples of how the Team Management Profile can be used appear below. They offer a glimpse of what is possible, but in no way demonstrate the full potential of the profile.

Case Study E

Mary Jones is an owner-manager of a small computer software company employing approximately 30 staff. She is a co-director along with her husband and another partner. Mary expressed concern about the way her company was being run. She tended to look after the office and general internal running of the company whilst the other two partners were heavily concerned with technical and promotional aspects of the business. The three partners tended to 'do their own thing' on day to day matters and there was little formal communication regarding operational matters. The three of them tried to hold equal status, and, as a result, no single one adopted the Managing Director role. Mary reported that there was a number of annoying mistakes made. For example, her husband and the other partner sent out inaccurate promotion material. On one occasion they planned an event on the Internet but the publicity material for it failed to state the time that the activity would take place. There were numerous other examples of poor attention to detail. Furthermore, Mary felt that many business contacts were frustrated because her company did not have a single director or manager who could act as a focal point for external communications. In many ways, internal communications suffered in the same way.

Mary's Team Management Profile indicated that her preferred way of working was introverted, practical, analytical and structured. Mary's major role therefore was Concluder-Producer. On studying her profile it struck her that there

---

were large differences between her approach to work and that of her husband and the other partner. She arranged for all three of them to have a profile produced. There was some resistance at first, particularly from her husband, but eventually profiles were produced and Mary felt able to discuss some of her concerns, pointing out to her colleagues that they had different ways of working. In fact, the initial success of the company was partly due to their differences, but what had happened was that growth had resulted in the need for greater co-ordination. The three agreed that Mary should take the role of Managing Director and that she would oversee events in the future. This agreement was based on the realisation that the partners had different strengths. Mary's major strength was that she was extremely practical and that she had an eye for detail. Her partners' major roles, on the other hand, were Creator-Innovator and Explorer-Promoter. This mixture of work preferences can result in an excellent partnership, providing a way is found to manage their differences.

The Margerison-McCann Team Management Profile provided a mechanism for the partners to discuss their differences. Previously, they had been unable or unwilling to do this. Following Mary's appointment as MD, both internal and external communications improved. In addition, since all communications went through her, the number of errors and omissions were reduced significantly.

The next case study is an example where a Managing Director was able to improve the relationships between himself and his management team through achieving greater mutual understanding of their different styles.

Case Study F

Albert is a Managing Director of an engineering company employing approximately 100 staff. Albert's profile identified him as having extroverted, creative, beliefs-oriented and flexible preferences. Albert's major role therefore is Creator- Innovator. There are six people on the Senior Management Team. Albert felt that his management team was frequently frustrated with the way he approached problems and issues. There was no open conflict, but problems arose over how decisions were made. Albert genuinely wanted to improve this situation. Various methods had been used previously to improve teamworking; for example, Belbin's Teamrole Inventory was used as a basis of a team workshop but little had altered. Albert then came across the Team Management Profile and arranged for the team members to complete the questionnaire. The results were illuminating in one major respect. All of the other managers had a strong preference for making decisions based on analysis rather than on beliefs. Albert was the opposite. In the resulting discussions many of the other managers expressed their relief. "I thought he was just being awkward," said one manager. Another stated, "that's why he is so stubborn." The team discussed this issue and they agreed that in the future, where possible, decisions would be a more shared responsibility. More importantly, however, the process helped the managers and Albert understand their own preferred ways of working and that of others. This greater understanding is the basis for improving work relationships and performance.

Conclusion

This chapter began with a discussion of why managers must constantly update their knowledge and skills, but at the same time be aware not to adopt the 'flavour of the month' in terms of management practices. The concept of management self-development is particularly useful and can be approached in various ways. In this chapter, four distinctive approaches have been described, and cases provided that demonstrate how these can be applied. The particular approach that a person might use depends

on a variety of factors, including cost, ease of use and how
appealing the particular method is to the user. The devices
described here are only tools to help the manager analyse their
skills and work preferences. What is important is that managers
are able to reflect on their behaviours, attitudes and values and
take appropriate courses of action to improve their own performance and that of their organisation. Very often this involves
managers moving out of their 'comfort zones' and developing
themselves in new and different ways. This is a real challenge
for managers, it has considerable opportunities but is also
fraught with many obstacles and dangers.

Notes

1. A copy of the Personal Competence Inventory can be
   obtained from: Wes Haydock, Bolton Business School, Deane
   Road, Bolton, Lancs. BL3 5AB.

2. The publishers of Margerison-McCann Team Management
   Systems are TMS Development International Ltd, 128
   Holgate Road, York   YO24 4FL.
   Website: www.tmsdi.com. E-mail: enquiry@tmsdi.com.

References

Adair, J, *Action Centred Leadership* (London: McGraw Hill) 1984.

Armstrong, M, *How to be an Even Better Manager* (London: Kogan Page) 1994.

Belbin, M, *Management Teams: Why they Succeed and Fail* (Oxford: Heinemann) 1981.

Blake, R R & J S Mouton, *The Managerial Grid* (Houston: Gulf) 1964.

Boak, G, *Developing Managerial Competencies: The Management Learning Contract Approach* (London: Pitman) 1991.

Bones, C, *The Self-Reliant Manager* (London: Routledge) 1994.

Connor, J & W Haydock, *Personal Competence Inventory* (Bolton: Bolton Business School Press) 1992.

Cotton, J, *The Theory of Learners* (London: Kogan Page) 1995.

Fayol, H, *General and Industrial Management* (London: Pitman) 1949.

Fletcher, C, "Appraisal: An Idea whose Time has Gone?" in J Billsberry (ed), *The Effective Manager: Perspectives and Illustrations* (London: Sage) 1996.

Grint, K "What's Wrong with Performance Appraisals? A Critique and a Suggestion" *Human Resource Management Journal* (1993) Vol. 3, No. 3, pp. 61-77.

Handy, C, *The Empty Raincoat* (London: Hutchinson) 1994.

Hannagan, T, *Management: Concepts and Practices* (London: Financial Times/Pitman Publishers) 1998.

Honey, P & A Mumford, *The Manual of Learning Opportunites* (Maidenhead: Honey) 1989.

Klemp, G O (ed.), "The Assessment of Managerial Competence" Report to the National Institute of Education (Washington DC) 1980.

Kolb, D, I Rubin & J McIntyre, *Organizational Psychology: An Experiential Approach* (New Jersey: Prentice-Hall) 1979.

Kolb, D, "Management and the Learning Process" in K Starkey, *How Organizations Learn* (London: Thompson Business Press) 1996.

Margerison, C & R McCann, *Team Management Systems: Practical New Approaches* (Gloucestershine: Management Books 2000) 1995.

Mintzberg, H, *Mintzberg on Management: Inside out Strange World of Organisations* (New York: The Free Press) 1989.

NFMED, *Occupational Standards for Managers* (London: NFMED) 1990.

Pearce, S & S Cameron, *Against the Grain* (Oxford: Butterworth Heinemann) 1997.

Pedlar, M, J Burgoyne & T Boydell, *A Manager's Guide to Self-Development* (London: McGraw Hill) 1986.

Pedlar, M, J Burgoyne & T Boydell, *Applying Self-Development in Organisations* (Hemel Hempstead: Prentice Hall) 1988.

Reddin, W J, *How to Make your Management Style More Effective* (London: McGraw Hill) 1987.

Tannenbaum, R & W H Schmidt, "How to Choose a Leadership Pattern" *Harvard Business Review* (1957) Vol. 36, No. 2.

Taylor, F, *Principles of Scientific Management* (New York: Harper and Row) 1949.

Woodcock, M & T Francis, *The Unblocked Manager* (Aldershot: Gower) 1996.

Chapter 3

TEAMWORKING IN A SMALL BUSINESS

Tony Scott

Introduction

Small businesses have a number of strengths that are the envy of larger organisations. Internal communication is generally straightforward. Since the number of employees is relatively small, there are few, if any, levels of management between operatives and the owner-managers. The business is often located on a single site, which means that the workforce works in close proximity to one another.

There is often a sense of community in small businesses. Business success as well as setbacks have almost immediate impact, and can be much more transparent than in larger, scattered, anonymous corporations. There is a tendency for all to share common goals. Success is celebrated together and there is bonding in adverse situations.

Thus, in a well-managed small business, a carefully selected group of employees can be welded into a flexible and effective team.

The downside of this situation is that a small business rarely employs specialists, unless their knowledge and skills are at the core of its business activity. Consequently, when the occasional requirement arises for specialist expertise, the organisation has to buy-in.

Selecting the provider of this expertise can be problematical. A bad choice can be very expensive and damaging to the business. Oftentimes the recommendation of a friend or reliable contact is preferred to tendering and selecting from a short-list, even though the latter is more objective.

Whatever the method of selection, the primary goal is to

make the best use of the external specialist and a subsidiary goal is to minimise the need to buy-in the expertise again in the future. This can lead to disputes about the scope of the service and the completeness and quality of what has been provided, including documentation and training.

Traditionally, the issues associated with externally resourced projects are addressed by tight client-provider contractual arrangements. The client may seek a fixed price, whereas the service provider will prefer a time and materials arrangement. From the outset there are likely to be defensive tactics to protect the differing interests of client and provider, which, if not handled properly, can descend into an adversarial situation.

An alternative approach has emerged in recent years. Central to it is the concept of Joint Development Teams (JDT), comprising clients and providers. A number of strategies and techniques have been developed to exploit the JDT concept. The Dynamic Systems Design Method (DSDM) is an example of a framework that incorporates these. Developed by a consortium of large and small businesses including every sector of industry, it has gained acceptance and is widely used in the UK, Europe, Australia and the Asia Pacific region. Intended initially for IT projects, where client requirements are often ill-defined or uncertain, it has general application to any project where there is a need for partnership between client and provider to ensure that business needs are met.

Goal

Before examining a framework that incorporates JDT and other strategies and techniques, we need to clearly identify the situations in which it may be useful.

Let us consider a case study.

Case Study A

DP, the owner-manager of a growing business that manufactures and sells uPVC windows is reviewing his business plan. Initially, the business was based on selling replacement windows for domestic properties – the fuel savings

---

---

*associated with double glazing and the reduced mainte-
nance cost of uPVC were the main features of promotional
literature and adverts. Price competition is fierce, recent
mild winters have blunted the effectiveness of a sales-pitch
based on reducing fuel costs and more and more new
houses already have doubleglazing. However, conservato-
ries have introduced a new sales opportunity that DP has
enthusiastically and successfully addressed.*

*DP feels that there are two developments that would
sustain the profitability and growth of the business.*

1. *Supplying (and perhaps fitting) windows for new properties, commercial as well as domestic, requires a different approach to marketing. New customers will be
   other businesses – builders and builders' merchants –
   instead of the public.*

2. *A bigger geographic area would increase the potential
   customer base but this requires a different approach to
   advertising and careful consideration of delivery costs
   and the number of fitters.*

*DP is inundated with advertising and approaches from
organisations trying to persuade him that an Internet web
page would help him sell his products. The cost isn't great
but DP feels unhappy about letting an outsider control the
design of the advert and the handling of enquiries. He is
concerned that some of those offering Internet access may
be technically competent with IT but understand little
about his business need for effective marketing.*

*He resolves to buy-in marketing and IT expertise to
address his wish to sell to the trade and widen his target
market.*

Thus, a project is to be undertaken which requires the expertise
of a specialist external to the core activity of the business, and
there is some uncertainty as to the deliverables and the work
involved in producing it.

There is a need to:

- make the best use of the skills of the external specialist;
- ensure that business requirements are clarified and met during the project;
- gain business benefit from the project at the earliest possible time;
- develop the skills of core employees so that they can continue and build on the project outcomes.

Key Features of an Approach using JDT

A method such as DSDM will encompass the following features.

1. A Joint Development Team in which team members' roles are clearly defined, with a high degree of self-direction (i.e. empowerment) as a partnership between client and provider.

2. Required business outcomes, defined by the executive sponsor of the project (e.g. the owner-manager), are delegated to the team of decision-makers on how the outcomes are achieved. The outcomes must indicate the quantitative and/or qualitative criteria by which success can be judged.

3. An incremental approach involving early identification of the business requirements that are most valued by the business, early delivery of these while further requirements are identified and addressed and continual 'requirements scrubbing' to eliminate or postpone features or activities that have low utility.

4. Time-boxes with immovable deadlines and prioritised deliverables that can be added to, or dropped from, a time-box according to their contribution to business benefits.

5. Differentiation between functional and non-functional aspects of the requirements so that any essential enabling features are clearly identified and included.

6. Use of prototyping to explore business requirements, develop and refine solutions and consolidate them into the business.

The prototypes are jointly planned by the client and provider, developed by the provider and then jointly reviewed to identify shortcomings and determine the utility of further development work.

7. Risk management. Throughout the project, the team actively considers the possibility of error and undertakes checking of accuracy and validity of deliverables according to the likely impact of error. As far as possible, the team makes every change reversible so that backtracking can be carried out. A 'no blame' philosophy is adopted, and details of mistakes and errors are communicated to the whole team so that they are not repeated.

Additional Benefits

The DSDM method accommodates situations that are initially ill-defined or uncertain. Instead of trying to prepare a detailed specification of requirements at the outset, the method incorporates a mechanism that allows clarification and 'migration' of requirements as the team investigates the situation, explores innovative solutions and gains experience. Control is left in the hands of the client by the technique of time-boxing and prioritisation by business benefit. This contrasts with more traditional methods where changes to the initial specification are considered a failure in the project definition phase.

The method recognises that getting it right the first time and 'zero defects' are desirable, but not always possible. Quality checking is matched to the business' sensitivity to inaccuracy and the procedures facilitate early identification of weakness and backtracking.

Progress is visible to the client because of their active participation in the team throughout the project. This gives earlier warnings of problems that could affect business activity external to the project.

Unlike most projects, deadlines are always met. The deliverables at the end of a time-box may exclude some of the planned functionality, but any omission will be that of least business value.

Overheads are lower because prototyping removes the need for client and provider to agree on a specification before development begins. There is less need for progress reports because of the empowerment of the team, the ongoing participation of the client and because schedule slippage and serious cost over-run are eliminated by time-boxing.

Acceptability and 'ownership' of the deliverables are not issues because the team includes clients who have been actively involved at every stage of design and review.

Critical Success Factors

There must be top-level commitment to the method. The owner-manager must adopt the role of executive-sponsor, defining what is to be done in the form of required business outcomes but leaving the 'how' to the team. In a small business, the owner-manager often finds it easy to resist the temptation to intervene because progress is visible and the client member of the team is well-known and trusted. On the other hand, an owner-manager's entrepreneurial nature may conflict with the need to delegate decision-making.

Empowering the team is equally important. Client members of the team must have sufficient knowledge and understanding of the business requirements of the project and its context, and be willing and able to think flexibly and innovatively and make decisions.

There must be client-provider trust so that the absence of detailed specification and a rigid contract does not stultify the behaviour of either partner.

JDT Roles

Dr Merideth Belbin, undertaking research at the Industry Training Research Unit and Administrative Staff College, Henley, hypothesised that:

- individuals are not good at everything;
- people are dependent on other people they work with;
- teams/groups have more to contribute than the individuals (1+1=3).

His research led to the identification of eight distinct team roles, and the conclusion that the roles must be fulfilled with little duplication and few gaps for the team to be effective. The suitability of individuals to fill the roles may be established by an appropriate questionnaire (such as the Margerison-McCann Team Managment Profile discussed in Chapter 2) that establishes their natural traits. The roles identified by Belbin are indicated below.

Role	Contribution
Co-ordinator	A good chairperson. Welcomes all contributors on their merits and without prejudice, clarifies goals, promotes decision-making, delegates well.
Sharper	Challenging, dynamic, thrives on pressure. Dislikes inertia, complacency, ineffectiveness or self-deception.
Innovator	Source of original/inspired ideas. Solves difficult problems, undertakes conceptual thinking.
Monitor-Evaluator	Seperates practical ideas from the others and keeps the team on the right track.
Implementer	Organises self and others, turns ideas into practical actions and schedules, meets deadlines.
Team-worker	Develops contacts outside the team, acquires resources, reponds positively to problems.
Resource Investigator	Develops contacts outside the team, acquires resources, responds positively to problems.

Completer- Finisher:	Progress-chaser. Searches out errors and omissions. Follows through and delivers on time.

Adapted from Belbin, Management Teams: Why they succeed or fail (Oxford:

Butterworth) 1996.

Below is a management perspective of the people's team roles offered by Constantine.

Role	Contribution
Co-ordinator	Controls team direction at the highest, strategic level. Moves the problem-solving forward by recognising strengths and weaknesses and making the best use of human and other resources.
Driver	Controls team direction at a detailed, tactical level. Defines things, steers and shapes group discussions and activities.
Originator	Provides leadership in ideas, innovating and inventing ideas and strategies, especially on major issues.
Monitor	Analyses problems from the practical point of view and evaluates ideas and suggestions so the team can make balanced decisions.
Implementer	Converts concepts and plans into work procedures and carries out group plans efficiently and as agreed.
Supporter	Builds on team members' strengths and underpins any shortcomings. Provides emo-

	tional leadership and fosters team spirit. Improves communications among team members.
Investigator	Explores and reports on ideas, developments and resources outside the group. Creates external contacts that may be useful to the group.
Finisher	Ensures that all necessary work is completed in all details. Seeks work that needs greater than average attention to detail and maintains the group's focus and sense of urgency.

Source: Constantine, Constantine on Peopleware (Englewood Cliffs, NJ: Yourdon Press) 1995.

This provides a more structured approach that facilitates planning the team membership, whereas Belbin's model is useful for analysing the strengths of available personnel.

Belbin's and Constantine's models address personal traits and the behavioural aspects of team roles. However, a JDT has a number of distinct requirements, and a more functional model is discussed below.

The situation that leads to a JDT project is such that there is a knowledge gap between client staff members of the team (who bring knowledge of the business and the business' requirements) and staff of the providing organisation (who have what might be termed 'technical' expertise). It is appropriate, therefore, to differentiate these roles.

The team may have to call upon additional expertise from outside the 'core' team. It is helpful to note this fact.

The project needs a 'champion' at the highest level, both for the project and for the method used. This is likely to be the owner-manager in a small business. The term 'executive sponsor' gives a good indication of the function.

As identified by Belbin and Constantine, there must be someone within the team with the vision and the capacity to offer innovative and unconventional solutions.

Techniques used by JDTs, such as facilitated workshops, need to be carefully managed, and it is helpful to have a team member with the specific role of facilitating these.

It is equally important that in the 'hot house' environment of workshops and prototyping, facts and decisions are recorded. Indeed, such records are essential to support the concept of backtracking. Thus, a record keeper role should be identified.

A final role, that of 'observer', is also suggested. This provides for non-participants at workshops, role-plays, etc. and ensures that the team is not thought of as elitist by the rest of the organisation.

The following summarises the roles that are appropriate to a JDT.

Role	Attributes	Contribution
Project Manager	Project planning and management skills. Skill with the techniques to be used by the team (e.g. facilitated workshops, prototyping). Business awareness. Technical awareness. Good communicator.	Project management. Task and people management.
Executive Sponsor	Ability to commit appropriate funds and resources. Seeks sound justification. Decisive. Business knowledge. Political awareness.	Champion the project and the method.
Visionary	Excellent awareness of business goals. Highly aware of technological possibilities. Good communicator.	Creative and innovative ideas.
Client Representative	Knowledge of the relevant business area goals and practices. Aware of organisational politics.	Knowledge of business and business requirements.

	High-level view of how the solution should support the business. Good communicator. Ability to disseminate knowledge and ideas. Access to client specialists as necessary.	
Client Specialist	Detailed and practical knowledge of specific business area. Ability to communicate knowledge and ideas.	Expertise and advice in specific business areas.
Provider Representative	Technical expertise. Experience of JDT techniques. Business awareness. Good communicator. Access to specialist providers as necessary.	Technical knowledge. Solutions to business requirements.
Specialist Provider	Expertise in specific technical areas. Ability to communicate and contextualise.	Expertise and advice in specific technical areas.
Facilitator	Excellent inter-personal skills. Excellent communication and presentation skills. Ability to be impartial. Competent in the workshop process. Business awareness.	Leads workshops and other group activity.
Scribe	Good listening and written communication skills. Business and technical awareness.	Keep records. Remind team of protocols.
Observer	Interest in business and technical areas being considered. Restraint.	Disseminate information and make suggestions through proper channels.

The Team Life Cycle

The nature of a JDT project in a small business is such that its members are likely to be brought together for the first time at the beginning of the project. It is important, therefore, to recognise the stages that the team must go through to reach maximum effectiveness and the likely pattern of behaviour as the project nears its end.

Maylor (1996) identifies six phases that a team is likely to encounter over the project's life cycle. These reflect the change in behaviour and effectivness of the team and are outlined below.

Stage	Characteristics
Collection	Bringing individuals together into a group to tackle a project or particular problem. The participants have a degree of eagerness and initial enthusiasm and generally rely on the authority and hierarchy to provide a degree of certainty in this uncertain environment. They will use this initial phase to establish themselves and find what is expected of them.
Entrenchment	As the group starts work they begin to find out where each other stands on various issues. The entrenchment comes when people arrive with preconceived ideas as to how the project should be proceeding and are unwilling to be persuaded of the merits of allowing the group to decide on the course of action. This phase can be very destructive and is generally fairly unproductive. The reasons for this unproductiveness are issues such as disillusionment with the goals of the project, competition for power or attention within the group or general confusion as to what tasks need to be done to complete the project.
Resolution/ Accommodation	The disagreements begin to be resolved, and characteristics, such as mutual trust, harmony, self-esteem and confidence, are seen. This is where the team starts to put the nega-

	tive social effects aside and move to being more productive.
Synergy	The output of the whole is greater than what would be obtained from the component parts (otherwise stated as $2 + 2 = 5$). This stage in the team life cycle is the peak of its effectiveness. Leadership is shared according to the agreed team roles, and there is a new motivation to complete the tasks at hand.
Break-up	If the group finishes the project before the project is complete, there can be problems in getting a new team to take up the remaining work. They will be expected to get up to speed very quickly and have an additional pressure on them.

Empowerment

A key element in JDT is the empowerment of the team. Byham provides a good working definition of empowerment:

> *A feeling of job ownership and commitment brought about through the ability to make decisions, be responsible, be measured by results, and be recognised as a thoughtful contributing human being rather than a pair of hands doing what others say.*[1]

Gilgeous (1997) discusses the implications of empowerment. Clearly, the roles of people within the organisation must be changed – by delegation of decision making, by the manager taking a facilitator role instead of directing subordinates, etc. However, not all staff will wish to take on more responsibility

---

1. Byham, W C, "Would you Recognise the Empowered Organisation if you Saw One?" *Tapping the Network Journal* (1992) Vol. 3, No. 2, pp. 10-13.

and the concomitant increase in stress, perhaps for no more pay. Some may welcome increased autonomy and the opportunity to demonstrate entrepreneurship and a capacity for innovation to gain a sense of achievement. Others may feel insecure and uncomfortable in a higher-profile position.

Client representatives must feel comfortable in an empowered team and must be selected and prepared for their team role. Equally, the owner-manager must be prepared to 'let go' of many decisions and this may lead to a feeling of loss of control and insecurity.

Unless the team is empowered, the bonding of the client and provider representatives into a team and the achievement of goals will be undermined.

JDT Workshops

An important technique associated with the JDT is that of facilitated workshops. The DSDM Consortium (1998) defines a Facilitated Workshop thus:

> *A facilitated workshop is a team-based information gathering and decision-making technique designed to accelerate business planning and development. It is an interactive communication technique involving experienced and empowered personnel working in one or more sessions run by an independent facilitator. A workshop is a process to be implemented when there is a requirement to make decisions, explore ideas and exchange knowledge to solve a business problem.*

The primary aim is to reach decisions that are mutually acceptable. There must be clear outcomes. The facilitator must ensure that the workshop focuses on meeting business requirements and seeking solutions rather than dwelling on problems, and avoids getting bogged down in technical detail. That is not to say that hazards and risks should be ignored; in fact, risk management (identification, assessment, avoidance, containment) are crucial to the process.

The fact that all stakeholders are 'sat round the table' has a number of potential benefits in that it:

- clarifies decisions and highlights disputes that must be referred to the executive sponsor;
- shortens the requirements definition phase;
- helps to eliminate features of questionable value;
- helps get the requirements right the first time;
- reduces organisational in-fighting.

The ground-rules for a facilitated workshop are:

- plan: define objectives, scope and deliverables;
- prepare: book facilities (see below), issue of background and specific pre-reading in good time, construct a realistic agenda;
- limit the participants to six to twelve people;
- start on time, keep to the timescale (time-box each agenda item);
- insist that everyone respects others' views;
- allow only one speaker at a time;
- adopt the principle that 'silence is assent';
- always work towards the objectives;
- conduct a 'wrap-up' session at the end of the workshop to confirm decisions and identify outstanding items.

The following schematic illustrates the key components of a facilitated workshop:

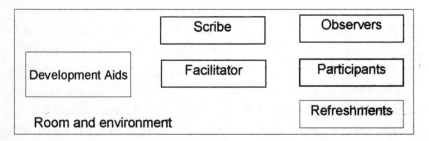

Properly run, a facilitated workshop will achieve good quality outcomes and participant satisfaction, there will be a better understanding of the business and technical issues, and it will have been possible to cut across organisational barriers and reduce the effects of politics, hidden agenda and conflicting needs.

There is a number of potential problems. Observers may not confine themselves to observing. The effectiveness of the workshop will be impaired if there are too many participants. People who are 'performers' may outshine 'doers'. It is the facilitator's responsibility to overcome these problems.

Facilitation Techniques

Fisher and Ury's book *Getting to Yes* provides helpful recommendations.

- Separate the people from the problem.

- Focus on people's interests rather than their positions.

- Invent options for mutual gain.

- Insist on using objective criteria.

Theory-W Software Project Management (Boehme & Ross, 1989) is also helpful.

1. Establish win-win preconditions:

   - Understand how people want to win.

   - Establish reasonable expectations on the part of all stakeholders.

   - Provide an environment that supports the project goals.

   - Match people's tasks to their win conditions.

2. Structure the win-win process:

   - Establish a realistic plan.

   - Use the plan to control the project.

   - Identify and manage the win-lose and lose-lose risks.

   - Keep people involved.

3. Structure the product:
   • Match product to people's win conditions.

Time-boxing

A time-box is an identified period of time within which certain tasks and outcomes will be acheived. In project management terms, these tasks and outcomes are referred to as deliverables.

The time-box technique is intended to give frequent acheivement of deliverables that meet business requirements. Thus, the business benefits from these while other, lower priority requirements are being worked on.

Effective use of the time-box techniques depends on empowerment. Clients and providers must agree on the scope and objectives of the time-box. Objectives should be expressed as deliverables and be based on the high-level business requirements of the project.

Once the deliverables are defined, the resource requirements are estimated and the time-box duration is calculated. The providers generally have greater expertise in estimation. Time-boxes should typically be between two and six weeks' duration. A major advantage of keeping time-boxes short is that it is easier to calculate the duration accurately.

At the deadline the clients will be primarily responsible for approving the deliverables produced in the time-box.

If during the period of the time-box it appears that the deadline will be missed, the time-box should be de-scoped. The team must agree on what deliverables are to be retained in the current time-box and which will be slipped back to a later time-box.

Requirements can slip, but the time-box deadline never does.

Any subsequent time-box containing dependent work cannot be started before the previous time-box is complete. This is because the previous time-box may not deliver all that was originally planned.

The time-boxing technique has the advantage of avoiding delayed implementation, forces the team to regularly consider business priorities, limits 'gold-plating' by the providers and controls 'feature creep'. Time-boxing provides good project control, but makes management more intense.

Care must be taken not to try to time-box inappropriate tasks such as project planning or those that have large downstream implications. The team must resist the temptation to sacrifice quality rather than deliverables.

Prototyping

Business prototypes can be used to:

- clarify and confirm business requirements;
- broaden the client's awareness of possible solutions that meet business requirements;
- confirm that details are correct for specific parts of the solution;
- try out solutions before putting in the additional work that makes them sufficiently robust for roll-out.

Prototyping speeds up the development process and increases user confidence that the right system is being built.

A prototype is just that – a prototype. A prototype need not be complete and tested with respect to all its related functional and non-functional requirements. However, in the context of the small business JDT, prototypes are intended to evolve into the final system.

The prototyping approach encourages incremental development. The first version of the solution is the basis for further development. More functionality and more non-functional features may be added as the business requirements change, or as staff gain experience and become more sophisticated.

Prototypes may take many forms. For example, it may be a business plan, preferably set up as a spreadsheet model so that the results of changing parameters can be easily observed, or it may be a story board or a role-play to explore a scenario. Both business and technical imperatives will drive the choice of prototyping tool.

Differentiating Functional and Non-functional Requirements

Well-designed business solutions should be simple, straightforward, easy to learn and understand and fun to use. If done well, the roll-out to other parts of the business will be easier, with staff requiring less training since they will already have a good understanding of the full capabilities of the solution.

In the early stages, a prototype may have a number of rough edges. This is both understandable and acceptable, because the team will have better-than-average capability to handle these; they have, after all, been specially chosen and trained.

The refinements that make a solution suitable for general use throughout the business are known as the non-functional requirements of the solution.

Ensuring that the non-functional requirements are met can be time consuming. It is important that the client representatives in the team understand this.

Refining the solution is often best done as an iterative process using the prototyping technique.

One aspect of the non-functional requirements is to check that the solution will function adequately in the live environment, even when competing for resources with other parts of the business. It may be necessary to simulate peak-time workload and see whether any 'bottlenecks' occur. The team should anticipate the issues that arise when the solution is used by other staff who may have less capability or motivation.

Another non-functional aspect of the solution is its capacity to handle exceptions and error conditions, periodic and occasional requirements. A common way of doing this is to set up a test scenario and role-play through it while changing different aspects of the scenario to see how the solution performs. This process ought to be automated or well documented as a script of sorts so that it can be easily repeated.

Managing the Prototyping Process

As a general rule, it is recommended that three processes be followed on a prototype:

- investigation to confirm the requirements and explore possible solutions;
- refinement to build on the comments and feedback;
- consolidation to confirm that requirements are fully met.

For each process the team should:

- consider what has to be achieved, how to do it and how long it should take;
- undertake the development work and testing;
- review using a walked-through, scripted demonstration or role play to identify and note any weaknesses, and decide whether further work on the prototype can be justified by the improvements in business benefits.

During the planning stage, the team must consider what functional and non-functional features need to be incorporated. They should decide on the relative priorities of the prototype's various components, using criteria based on their contribution to business requirements or their vitalness to the overall solution. 'Must haves' should be tackled first and lesser parts will be dealt with if time is available. 'MoSCoW' rules are used in the DSDM method – Must, Should, Could, Won't – as a simple but effective prioritisation system.

The team must also make sure that it will be possible to backtrack and must decide what approach will be adopted for testing the acceptability of the solution.

As far as possible, prototypes are developed collaboratively by clients and providers. However, clients will probably take a back seat when dealing with non-functional requirements. Conversely, the providers will take a back seat when decisions are being made about appropriateness to meet business requirements.

The review stage has two aims:

- to ensure that the team is following the right track;
- to get the clients to buy into completed and future work.

During the review, the team will decide:
- which objectives have been met successfully;
- if there are any shortcomings, which need to be dealt with by another process, and which can be safely postponed to another time-box (or project) in order to meet the time-box's deadline.

Risks

The plan should not be allowed to slip unless significant problems arise, e.g. unexpected and dramatic changes in scope. Some problems may require temporarily halting all activity while the project direction is rethought. The ability to backtrack easily is especially relevant at such a time.

The most common threats to project success are:
- feature creep;
- gold-plating requirements;
- short-changed quality;
- overly optimistic schedules (e.g. delayed approval, external supplier promises);
- inadequate design;
- silver bullet syndrome (assuming a person or technique is infallible);
- pioneering (research-oriented) development – new tools/techniques;
- badly selected or poorly prepared personnel.

The team should adopt a risk resolution strategy that seeks to:
- buy information about the risk so that uncertainty is reduced;
- avoid the risk;
- transfer the risk to another part of the project where the impact is less;
- eliminate the root cause;
- accept the risk (if impact is small compared with avoidance cost);

- develop contingency plan;
- publicise risk;
- remember the risk.

A technique for ensuring that the team continually reflects on project risks is described by McConnell (1996):

Weekly 'Top 10 Risk List'				
This week's ranking	Last week's ranking	Weeks on list	Risk	Resolution progress
1				
2				
3				
4				
5				
6				
7				
8				
9				
10				

Conclusion

Small businesses occasionally need specialist expertise to help them with specific projects. Concerns arise when, in determining the scope of the service required by the business, there is insufficient technical 'know how' in the small firm to provide a detailed specification. The use of a Joint Development Team approach can improve the chances of success, provided that a number of key points are remembered.

- The provider of the specialist knowledge needs to be committed to a partnership with the small business.

- The small business need to commit staff to the project in order to develop internal skills.

- Staff needs to be given the responsibility to make decisions, the owner-manager needs to 'let go' of these areas of control and empower the staff working on the project.

- The project team needs to work within time-boxes to ensure that tasks are completed on an incremental and frequent basis.

Finally, the team must also ensure that the need to meet business priorities is an integral part of the process and that any prototype solution will lead to improved success.

References

Ansoff, H I (ed.), *Business Strategy* (London: Penguin) 1969.

Belbin, R M, *Management Teams: Why they Succeed or Fail* (Oxford: Butterworth) 1996.

Boehme Barry & R Ross, *Theory-W Software Project Management: Principles and Examples (IEEE Transactions on Software Engineering SE-15)* (July 1989) pp. 902-916.

Byham, W C, "Would You Recognise the Empowered Organisation if You Saw One?" *Tapping the Network Journal* (1992) Vol. 3, No. 2, pp. 10-13.

Constantine, Larry, *Constantine on Peopleware* (Englewood Cliffs, NJ: Yourdon Press) 1995.

Fisher, Roger & William Ury, *Getting to Yes* (New York: Penguin Books) 1981.

Gilgeous, Vic, *Operations and the Management of Change* (London: Pitman) 1997.
Maylor, Harvey, *Project Management* (London: Pitman) 1996.

McConnell, Steve, *Rapid Development* (Redmond: Microsoft Press) 1996.

Chapter 4

BUSINESS GROWTH AND FAILURE

Peter Moran and Frank Sutton

Introduction

This chapter attempts to analyse two overlapping phenomena. It proposes to examine the mainstream approaches to business growth critically and to point out the organisational and behavioural pathogens that may cause businesses to fail. These two themes meet at a tangent where a 'dash for growth' has exhausted an enterprise's resource base to the point where it can no longer sustain itself and ceases to trade. At the macro level, the growth of small and medium-sized enterprises (SMEs) is applauded as contributing to employment, wealth generation and domestic standards of living. At the micro level, 'growing' the business may not be without considerable personable angst and financial risk.

When analysing the growth of small businesses, there are a number of caveats that have to be remembered. This is that not all businesses wish to grow larger and there are some very powerful reasons for this. The first is exemplified by the 'lifestyle business', organisations set up under the control of one (or a few) individuals, usually in desirable surroundings, providing products or services for narrow market niches where the potential for growth is ignored studiously. These businesses perhaps grow up to the point where tax efficiencies are maximised, or where most family members are gainfully employed.

The second is to recall that there are many ways of calculating firm size. These include number of employees, net asset value, floor space, turnover, profitability, market share, complexity/dispersion of operating sites, etc. Not all these indices are mutually compatible and over time, the emphasis may change from one to another. For example, it is likely that the capital expenditure required to develop the organisation's infrastructure will reduce profitability. Hence, net asset value may rise whilst profitability falls. Paradoxically, an inappropriate attempt to grow may induce failure as financial obligations outstrip cash flow and readily available lines of credit to maintain sufficient liquidity.

The third is to bear in mind that each SME attempting to grow is located in a specific context, with different owner-managers, business networks, access to financial support, business expertise and guidance etc, operating across a wide range of industrial and service sector categories. Of those that seek growth, different trajectories may be possible. For example, those offering computer-related products and services may be capable of very rapid rates of development, whilst others in different areas of activity may not. Beyond these caveats are two main approaches to conceptualising growth. The first are 'stage' models of growth, related to the notion of an Organisational Life Cycle (OLC), whilst the second has centred on small firm development as driven by the entrepreneurial personality.

Stage Models

Models encompassing the notion of an OLC utilise a biological metaphor that suggests organisations are born, grow and mature. The OLC dictates that internal structure and systems become more prevalent and elaborate as size increases. Haire adroitly adopts the biological theme by suggesting: "A deer cannot grow as big as an elephant and still look like a deer; it has to look something like an elephant to support an elephant's mass."[1]

Over the years, a number of OLC frameworks have been developed by Schumpeter (1934), Urwick (1948), Steinmetz (1969), Greiner (1972), Churchill and Lewis (1983), Miller and Freisen

---

1. Haire, M, "Biological Models and Empirical Histories of the Growth of Organisations" in M Haire (ed.), *Modern Organisation Theory* (New York: John Wiley) 1959.

(1984), Flamholz (1986) and Scott and Bruce (1987). Later models adopt a stage approach. For example, Churchill and Lewis suggest:

Existence ➤ Survival Success ➤ Take Off ➤ Resource Maturity

The model Scott and Bruce suggest is as follows:

Inception ➤ Survival ➤ Growth ➤ Expansion ➤ Maturity

Each stage is accompanied by explanatory text. Rather than proffer all the details of each one in turn, take as an example the five-stage model of Miller and Freisen (1984). The first stage is birth, wherein small young firms attempt to establish themselves through innovation. The second is growth, departmentalising the business with more formal structures. They then move into maturity as stable efficient firms, but where increased bureaucracy stifles innovation, followed by decline (at stage four). Rather puzzlingly, the fifth stage is labeled 'revival' (achieved by the adoption of a market-based divisional structure permitting greater innovation to restore the company's fortune). Failure or exit surely deserves to be an option here. Not all basket case companies that encounter decline manage to escape the vortex of forces that try to pull them under. Of the models considered here, only Churchill and Lewis explicitly include a 'fold' option at each stage, acknowledging the possibility of business failure. However, any discourse as to why this occurred is omitted.

Greiner's (1972) model offers more promise in searching for an explanation of business failures. His model associates each stage of growth with a specific and dominant managerial or organisational crisis. The implication is that the resolution of each problem is necessary before proceeding to the next stage. The stage 'crisis' and 'solutions' stages are illustrated below.

Figure 1: Greiner's Stage Model Crises versus Stage Model Solutions

Growth Stage	Stage Crisis	Solution
Entrepreneurial	Creativity and leadership crisis.	Strong leadership/vision.
Collective	Need for delegation and control.	Add internal systems.
Formalisation	Too much red tape.	Develop teamwork.
Elaboration	Need for revitalisation.	a) streamline; return to small company thinking; b) continued maturity; c) decline.

Source: Greiner (1972)

Business Failure

Most small business start-ups do not make it past the entrepreneurial stage. Daft (1995: 177) cites the work of Land and Jarman in the US that suggests that 84 per cent of businesses that make it past the first year mark still fail within five years because their founders have not mastered the "vision thing" and the leadership qualities required to implement such vision are lacking. In common with business growth, failure (and failure proneness) is very difficult to measure with any degree of accuracy. Murphy suggests two definitions: "A business can be said to have failed when it is disposed of, or sold, or liquidated with losses to avoid further losses"; failure is defined as "the condition of the firm when it is unable to meet its financial obligations to its creditors in full. It is deemed to be legally bankrupt and is usually forced into an insolvency liquidation".[2]

Murphy qualifies these statements by adding the rider:

> *...the term business failure is variously translated as 'death of a business', 'ceasing to trade', 'deregistering from VAT', exit', 'bankruptcy' and 'insolvency'. Each term is not simply to be treated as a euphemism for failure. These terms reflect an intimate relationship with the data from which they are extracted. 'Exit', for example, may reflect an owner selling a business prior to retirement. If a 'good' price is achieved, this can hardly be labeled as 'failure'.*

Although hard data (e.g. VAT registrations and deregistrations) have to be handled with care, interpretative definitions of failure, which may or may not be tagged to the financial performance of the enterprise, are much more difficult to tease out. Indeed, they may be inexplicable or incapable of wider application outside specific owner-manager contexts, if at all. These may be very subjective, emotive judgements rooted in the psyche and behaviour of the individual business owner. They may be presented as (perceived?) failure to meet (self-imposed) targets that are not feasible in the first place.

This is supported in some of the literature, which suggests that entrepreneurs have a need for an internal locus of control (Rotter, 1966) and a very strong need for achievement (McClelland, 1961). This poses a number of difficulties in investigating the subject that include:

- Entrepreneurs may not be aware of their individual psychological drives that are pathogenic to their business.
- If they are aware of them, they may be unwilling to disclose or discuss them.

---

2. Murphy, M, *Small Business Management* (London: Pitman) 1994, p.23.

- Revisiting the causes of failure may be extremely painful for them.
- It is common for other stakeholders to conduct the post mortem and this may identify the prime causes of failure or otherwise.

An example of the latter is a study by Birley and Niktari (1995) that asked 486 bankers and accountants to give the reasons for client failure. Eighty-seven individual reasons were listed as contributing to the failure of an owner-managed firm. These were reduced to two dozen themes listed below.

Figure 2: Themes of failure

1. Capital structure.	13. Quality.
2. Management team.	14. Adverse publicity.
3. The economy.	15. Ill health.
4. Customer diversity.	16. Partnership problems.
5. Financial management.	17. Obsolescence.
6. Owner attitudes.	18. Reliance on grants.
7. Rising costs.	19. Family succession.
8. Lack of planning.	20. Legislation.
9. Pricing.	21. Cost of money.
10. Suppliers.	22. Personnel problems.
11. Marketing	23. Fire, flood.
12. Growth.	24. Industrial injury.

Source: Birley and Niktari (1995)

Although it appears that there may be direct connections between some of these factors, this list serves to underline the point made previously that the causes of failure may only be understood through an insight into the complexity and dynamics of specific contexts of failure. Significantly, two thirds of those who responded to Birley and Niktari's study, when asked, "Could the failure have been avoided?" replied "Yes". In their view, many businesses had been launched with a weak business concept and a lack of planning. That "basket-case" businesses fail is nothing new; however, understanding this simple axiom does not advance our understanding of it.

Frameworks for Understanding Business Failure

The academic study of business failure has made a number of different frameworks for closer analysis of the subject available. Weitzel and Jonnson (1989) have provided a stage model of business decline in counterpoint to the OLC models of growth and development outlined above. Argenti (1976) plotted business failure over longitudinal trajectories whilst Keasey and Watson (1986, 1991) review progress towards predicting the failure of small firms. Although published some time ago, Berryman's (1983) survey of the literature on small business failure and bankruptcy remains a good starting point outlining exogenous, behavioural and managerial factors.

Miller (1990) has suggested that organisational success and failure are closely linked – that the strength and success of outstanding companies leads them towards dogma, ritual and excess, over-specialisation and over-confidence. He refers to this as the Icarus Paradox, i.e. that the abilities of organisations to succeed contain the seeds of failure as inappropriate strategies are pursued. These are categorised as faulty trajectories that encompass focusing, venturing, inventing and decoupling.

The *focusing trajectory* involves crafts people who become 'tinkerers'. Such leaders place obsessive and excessive emphasis on quality, but in indulging this behaviour, they lose sight of the importance of satisfying customer requirements. Over-engineered, over-priced quality products result from a bureaucratic adherence to quality that dominates all other considerations. The *venturing trajectory* results from the dominance of "aggressive managers with ambitious goals, immense energy and an uncanny knack for spotting lucrative niches of the market".[3] They are imaginative, have initiative and are prepared to take risks. They also require sensitive information systems to track the perfor-

---

3. Miller, D, "The Icarus Paradox" (1990) in C A Carnell (ed.), *Strategic Change* (Oxford: Butterworth Heinemann) 1997, p.85.

mance of their expansive operations. If they move from "builders" to "imperialists", they rush into growth, incurring large amounts of debt while possibly lacking the expertise in new sectors of operation. They acquire companies that they cannot "sharpbend" and become failure-prone.

The *inventing trajectory* revolves around pioneer inventors who become "escapists" pursuing a "technological nirvana", producing products that are too advanced for the times, too impractical and over-priced. This results from the promotion of technological goals above market or profit goals. The *decoupling trajectory* features sale/marketing leaders who develop highly successful branded products, leading them to believe that they can sell almost anything. A bureaucratic approach strangles adaptation until "the leader is decoupled from [the] company, the company from its markets and the product lines and divisions from each other".[4]

Miller's (1993) work on the 'architecture of simplicity' develops the notion that success can initially be attained by a reductionist approach to business and a narrow focus on a single theme, issue or activity, such as quality, marketing or innovation. However, the price for ignoring the heterogeneous complexity of business is ultimately failure. Miller's work (1990, 1993), although providing useful insights into business failure, could be interpreted as the result of adopting faulty strategy. This is problematic in the translation of his meaning for small businesses, as Smallbone (1990) suggests that the biggest precursor of failure in small firms is inattention to strategy (not that an inappropriate strategy is developed, but rather, that there is *no* strategic plan).

Until the wider issue of entrepreneurial/owner-manager behaviour is considered, this can be understood from a rational standpoint as incongruent corporate governance. In this realm, rationality is not always in the forefront. It is possible to observe behavioural patterns that seem at odds with the context in which they occur, or perhaps the context has altered whilst belief and behav-

---

4. *Ibid.*, p. 87.

iour patterns have remained constant. Which is the given and which is the variable does not matter – both precipitate failure proneness.

Frog Types as a Metaphor for Failure-prone Managers

Villiers (1989) suggested that if a frog is taken from a pond and dropped into a pan of boiling water it senses the change in the environmental conditions immediately and jumps out. If, however, pond water temperature is gradually heated to boiling point, the incremental rise in temperature is so gradual that the frog fails to sense the change and will perish. In a small business sense, environmental changes must be monitored continually; an increase in competition, rising interest rates, skill shortages, difficulties in the supply chain, falling sales, increased inventory costs, etc. all represent a rise in temperature within the boiled frog metaphor.

Richardson *et al.* (1994) developed this metaphor into a typology of failure-prone frog types, covering both large and small businesses. As the former are beyond the scope of this book, only the latter are incorporated here. Predating Richardson's contribution is the work of Kets De Vries and Miller (1984), which suggests that specific organisational neuroses exist that stem largely from the organisational behaviour of those running the enterprise. These "neurotic organisations" can be compulsive, depressive, paranoid, schizoid or dramatic. In the case study below, both these metaphorical frameworks for understanding "anti-entrepreneurial" behaviour contain the seeds of failure-proneness.

An Entrepreneur at the Rubicon: Success or Failure?

Academic work in the field of small business management and entrepreneurship is beset by difficulties, and both are contested terms. As summarised elegantly by Chell, "the argument concerning the characteristics of small businesses and their owners is more complicated than might first appear, because it is entirely dependent upon the definition of what constitutes an entrepreneur, and what typifies a small business".[5] Without

---

5. Chell, E, "The Entrepreneurial Personality: A Few Ghosts Laid to Rest" *International Small Business Journal* (1985) Vol. 3, pp. 47-59.

regurgitating the proffered terms in full, suffice it to say that there are almost as many definitions of entrepreneurship and small businesses as there are authors on the subject(s). We borrow Beaver and Jennings' (1995) definition of an entrepreneur as one who is capable of "achieving and sustaining competitive advantage". Defining 'small' business engages relative and interpretative faculties on behalf of authors and readers alike.

Likewise, the definition of 'success' also lies within the interpretative paradigm. In addition to the visible, rational, calculable bank of financial indicators are the subjective emotions of 'feeling successful'. In this context, each entrepreneur has their own specific, intuitive (and usually hidden) set of indices by which they measure their own performance, that of their employees and their overall 'success' in business dealings. Anomalies arise when entrepreneurial activity appears to diverge markedly from traditional notions of (strategic) rational management purported to deliver 'business success'. Notwithstanding these problems, this case study profiles a successful male entrepreneur (known here by the pseudonym Jack), which focuses in particular on the nature of management within a small business situated in southern England.

It is also intended to be reflexive in that it enquires into the paradox that his current business success may contain the seeds of future failure-proneness. We attempt to adapt and deploy the frog metaphor developed by Villiers (1989), Handy (1991) and Richardson *et al.* (1994) as a perspective for interpreting some predictive indicators of failure-proneness. Presented in tandem is an analysis of Jack's business strategy, located within the sharp-bending framework developed by Grinyer, Mayes and McKiernan (1988).

Case Study A

Jack is nearly 60. More than 40 years ago, he left school without any formal qualifications and secured a job as a labourer. Thereafter, he joined a manufacturing company supplying the construction sector and rose to the position of foreman. He left to become a wagon driver at another company and soon became the transport manager. Now he owns the controlling interest of a plumbers' merchant that encompasses a manufacturing division and a transport operation. Other directors own the remainder of the business but take no part in running it. Jack decided to set up in the plumbing sector because he believed he could outperform the organisation that employed him. In common with many other business start-ups, the early days were hard. In the past he took nothing other than a subsistence wage from the business for the first years of operation and early financial difficulties are now recalled with some pride. The combined turnover for the constituent businesses is now approximately £18 million per annum. At the time of writing, several diversification ventures are under active consideration, including the provision of specialist products to sports clubs.

Jack the leader

Jack is a large, powerful man. Many employees consider him autocratic to the point of being dictatorial. Employee empowerment is not on his agenda. He is inclined to fearsome outbursts and strong language towards employees whom he considers to be "slacking", and the great majority of his employees are over-awed by him. Managers of this diverse enterprise are not involved in the strategic decision-making process – Jack is very much a loner and he is the sole decision-maker. His managers are expected to respond to instruction rather than develop initiative. There is no scope for employee 'experimentation' in devising new solutions to business problems. Jack seeks conformity to his own high standards of performance and commitment from his managers. Any (perceived) failure on their part upsets Jack to such a degree that they neither recover nor survive in his employment. Unconsciously, he utilises his physical presence and fear as effective devices in running the business.

Jack has a keen grasp of the importance of cash flow and basic control questions are constantly posed, such as, "What is the bank balance today? How much have we invoiced today? How much do we owe today?" He is fanatical about the accuracy of paperwork and the implementation of his standards to the extent that when an employee borrowed a small amount of money to purchase a computer (to work on company business at home outside normal office hours), Jack queried the transaction and enquired why interest had not been charged. Itemised telephone bills are checked line by line, all invoices are double checked and the issue of credit notes to customers prompts rigorous investigation. In this regard, Jack demonstrates the neurotic style characterised by Kets De Vries and Miller (1984: 24-25) as the compulsive leader who is characterised as seeking perfectionism, a preoccupation with trivial details, relationships seen in terms of dominance and submission. He also exhibits an inability to relax.

Jack works very hard: long hours are common and the key drivers appear to be maintaining an internal locus of control (Rotter, 1966) and avoiding failure. Reticent to trust the judgement of others, Jack neither invests authority in or delegates tasks to his managers. By contrast, as his business interests grow (and possibly diversify), models of the organisational life cycle (Greiner, 1972; Quinn & Cameron, 1983) suggest the need to extend and reinforce organisational architecture with functional specialists in clearly defined managerial roles with delegated powers.

The business is now capable of sustaining a standard of living for Jack and his family above average levels, but this has not always been the case. During the recession of the early-1990s, which dealt a hefty blow to the entire construction sector and when Jack's business was less profitable, he paid himself a minimal basic salary. Last year his total remuneration reached executive levels comprised a basic salary and profit-related bonuses. This reflects Jack's belief that there should be no upper earnings limit, providing that high profitability is achieved. To instil this ethos in others, salaries can be almost doubled through profit share payments. The Sales Director, for example, is paid the same basic salary plus a bonus, which has the potential to double his income if profit targets are achieved. The expanding financial status of the business is evidenced by the growth in turnover from circa £5 million in 1989 to approximately £18 million at present, with pre-tax profit margins of between 6 to 7 per cent. Hence, Jack is not extravagant in remunerating himself.

A restraining influence in this regard is his wife, who appears to regard naked materialism as unacceptable. Once when Jack paid himself more than she thought was "fair", she upbraided him and suggested that a portion of this sum might have been better spent had it been shared out among other employees. Jack also eschews ostentatious trappings sometimes associated with a successful entrepreneur. For example, his car is second hand with a diesel engine for economy. His managers are also provided with low mileage second hand cars and he insists that they, too, are diesel powered.

Jack has no hobbies per se. However, he lives on a small holding populated by quasi-domesticated animals and, apart from his business and family, this is his only interest. He dislikes taking holidays, but these are "arranged" for him. He prefers to spend time on his smallholding when not working. His house is modestly furnished and he expresses a vehement dislike of extravagant environments. Jack would prefer to lead a lifestyle based on self-sufficiency with regard to food, power, heat, etc.

Jack the sharpbender

Sharpbenders are defined by Grinyer et al. as "companies which have been in decline relative to their competitors, which have then exhibited a marked, and often dramatic improvement in performance; and which have sustained that high relative performance over a reasonable period of time and so are now regarded as outstanding in their industries".[6] Jack started business on his own account on one site and quickly acquired another two. Having established a profitable base in this area of activity, Jack displayed his entrepreneurial nature, refusing to rest on his laurels, and instead acquired other related businesses for very little (usually because they were bankrupt or close to it at the time of acquisition), turning them around into profitable businesses. The manufacturing division was added to his business interests in this fashion – for £750 he purchased the bankrupt company in the early, 1990s, which generated a recent profit in excess of £100,000 net. Similarly, he obtained the haulage operation for a sum just large enough to clear the debts of the existing owner. After he bought it, he recovered the debts that had eluded the previous owner and it generated a net profit of £60,000 in the first year.

His latest diversification involved the acquisition of another business for £250,000, which made no profit in the first year but contributed almost half this investment to the group after allowing for exceptional costs, which included one-off costs, such as redundancies. The growth of his business interests has been entirely self-funded until the purchase of this latest acquisition. At that point the bank granted him an overdraft facility approaching £0.5 million without the formalities of preparing business plans, cash flow projections, and so forth. He has currently drawn less than 25 per cent from the overdraft facility.

This appears congruent with Kets De Vries and Miller's (1988: 24-25) postulation that compulsive leaders display a predilection to avoid being at the mercy of events and to

---

6. Grinyer *et al.*, *Sharpbenders: The Secrets of Unleashing Corporate Potential* (Oxford: Blackwell) 1988, p. 2.

> *be in control. Equally, they suggest that this type of leader*
> *has attendant behavioural characteristics that can prove*
> *dangerous: an inward orientation, indecisiveness and*
> *postponement and difficulties in seeing the 'big picture'.*
> *Jack prevaricates between wishing to see his businesses*
> *grow and a simultaneous capacity for risk-aversion and a*
> *wish for his commercial concerns to gain size and strength*
> *whilst remaining within his existing 'comfort zone'.*
> *Making these decisions worries him considerably and in*
> *an attempt to see the 'big picture' with greater clarity, he*
> *has involved Frank as a consultant to assist in running the*
> *company.*

Jack the Frog?

It may appear odd that we are attempting to apply the failure-prone frog metaphor to a successful businessman. Jack does, however, display pronounced compulsive leader type behaviour and this may prove dysfunctional in the long-term. His leadership style, which has so far generated success, may precipitate failure-proneness in the future. Richardson *et al.* (1994) has presented the failure-prone organisation's matrix reproduced in Table 1 below.

Table 1: Failure-prone organisation's matrix

Small Organisation Type	Big Organisation Type	Frog Type
The hard-working, introverted family firm.	The (s)lumbering giant.	Boiled frog.
The ambitious entrepreneur.	The conglomerate king-maker.	Drowned frog.
The small firm flash.	The money-messing megalomaniac.	Bull frog.
The failed start-up.	The big project failure.	Tadpole.

Source: Richardson et al. (1994)

The boiled frog (Villiers, 1989) is typified by the business leader who fails to adapt to changing environmental conditions or, at the earliest stages of decline, refuses to accept that there is a crisis to be addressed. The time period for failure is approximately twenty years.[8] Despite their hard work ethic, the proportions of the changes required to rescue the business or lack of adequate finance to achieve a sharpbend eventually overwhelm such leaders. Jack works hard, but his business has been in existence for more than twenty years and as yet there are no apparent signs of corporate decay. He is constantly looking for new business opportunities and threats to existing operations.

The bullfrog in the SME context is the small firm flash, usually male, who 'milks' the organisation beyond its ability to sustain an extravagant lifestyle for its leader. No attention is paid to the organisational architecture. Many of the generic management tasks are either ignored or delegated to someone else, as time spent on such activities deprives the small firm flash of opportunities to show off, indulge the drive for self-gratifications of various kinds and generally have a good time funded by someone else. Upon the collapse of this business, the small firm bullfrog displays a tendency to favour 'serial' business failure, setting up one business after another as they fail in domino fashion. Jack is not extravagant or ostentatious, as witnessed by the fact that he does not pay himself beyond that which can be borne by the company and refused to buy a 'flash' car when the opportunity presented itself. He definitely does not delegate responsibility to others. The tadpole metaphor can also be disregarded, as Jack's business is not a failed 'start-up'.

The drowned frog leader type, the ambitious entrepreneur in the small business context, is partially applicable. Jack displays some, rather than all, of the characteristics accredited to the drowned frog, albeit in a diluted form. The drowned frog leader is often autocratic, brimming with ideas and characterised by a forceful approach. He seldom listens to views (or advice) that are opposed to his own. Jack displays this behaviour. Managers

---

7. Richardson, *et al.,* "Understanding the Causes of Business Failure Crises: Generic Failure Types: Boiled Frogs, Drowned Frogs, Bullfrogs and Tadpoles" *Management Decision* (1994) Vol. 32, No. 4, pp. 9-22.

who have challenged him, or indeed upset him in other ways, such as perceived poor performance, have been dispensed with. He does take advice from Frank, but this is proffered and usually (but not always) accepted in the context of a different power relationship. Frank is neither directly employed by him nor dependent upon him as a sole source of income. Nobody from within the group has aspired to or achieved the post which Frank now 'enjoys', encompassing the roles of trusted confidant, father confessor, sounding board for new business proposals and occasional adversary/devil's advocate.

The ambitious entrepreneur is constantly seeking growth – his early organisation is successful within a very short period of time and this encourages new projects. Notwithstanding the fact that Jack has been expanding his business interests for 30 years, some similarities remain. Jack's bankers provided a considerable overdraft facility not on the basis of soundly devised business plans or cash projections, but on the strength of his past performance and reputation as a successful entrepreneur.

Perhaps the most salient characteristic of the drowned frog leader is expansion into areas that are only remotely connected with the business leader's key strength, his detailed grasp and understanding of the particular market niche that nourished the original area of business activity. New business developments are accompanied by increased capital requirements, which, in this case, are readily available from financial institutions. Furthermore, his managerial attentions are distracted from the central 'lily pad' by these new ventures, and this renders him more failure-prone. To date, Jack's key market niche has been the plumbers' merchants and related businesses. He has now been offered a large sum for his stake in the plumbing business and he is currently considering whether to accept or reject this approach. The outcome may prove the acid test of Jack's potential for avoiding or becoming failure-prone.

If he accepts the bid, this will generate the necessary cash to expand into other commercial arenas, some of which are already under active surveillance. This will be difficult, but by divesting the plumbing operation, enough of his time and energy will be freed to permit him to concentrate on these new ventures. If he rejects the bid and decides to retain control over the plumbing business, whilst simultaneously continuing to pursue aggressive growth targets, this may render him failure-prone and place him within the drowned frog leader category, as his attentions are distracted from the central 'lily pad'.

Jack is a very successful entrepreneurial businessman, building his business over three decades. Success has not come suddenly, nor has the readiness of financial institutions to support his attempts to grow. He works very hard, insists that others in his employ do likewise and keeps a very tight reign on cash flow. He does not remunerate himself excessively and is prepared to trim his cloth when the business struggles to generate profit. There are, however, a number of behavioural traits that are resonant with the venturing trajectory. He is dominant, aggressive, prepared to take risks, has huge reserves of energy and sets ambitious goals. He is not yet an 'imperialist', but is examining growth opportunities in lucrative market niches, some of which are arguably beyond the scope of his current expertise.

He cannot yet be labelled failure-prone, but the strength of his determination to succeed and avoid failure may, ironically and paradoxically, prove to be a key weakness. He already exhibits most of the personality traits categorised by Kets De Vries and Miller (1984) as those of the compulsive leader. Some of the attendant pitfalls associated with this type of business leader are emerging: a predisposition towards bureaucratic inflexibility which lends itself to dysfunctionalism and discontent (although this is concealed from Jack) among middle managers resulting from their lack of influence and inability to display initiative.

Unless the 'success' factors Jack values are surfaced and made explicit, it is unlikely that the work of these managers will satisfy him. Although Jack does not dovetail perfectly into any of the failure-prone 'frog' types outlined by Richardson *et al.*, he is perhaps closest to the drowned frog – the over-ambitious entrepreneur. Again there is a paradox here – his constantly high levels of labour and anxiety are expended not to permit the fruits of the high life to be consumed, but perhaps in an attempt to approach the unattainable idyll of self-sufficiency. If he measures his success against this criterion, a positive correlation is highly unlikely, as the end point of complete independence (and control of one's own life) cannot be achieved and he will be destined to remain dissatisfied.

The decision of whether to retain the plumbing business or dispose of it has become a crossroads for Jack. If he sells and uses the capital to fund business ventures in related fields, his continued rise (or stability at least) may be assured, *ceteris paribus*. If he retains control over it and pushes forward with other projects, he risks becoming more aligned with the failure-prone drowned frog as the characteristics of the compulsive leader become more pronounced. The dissatisfied entrepreneur is at the Rubicon.

Although it is impossible to generalise about the failure (or success) orientations of individual SMEs and their owners from one case study, other sources point to the growing problem of company failure. "Data from CCN, the Nottingham-based credit investigation agency, show there are more than 300,000 serial failures – directors with more than one failed company behind them. This is just over 10 per cent of the 2.6 million company directors on its register. Of these, 4,000 have ten or more failed companies behind them".[8] Further, "the number of directors disqualified from taking any part in the management of a UK company has soared by 18 per cent. In the first six months of last year [1997] the courts banned 1,040 directors. This year [June 1998] the figure has already jumped to 1,267".[9]

---

8. Cohen, N, "Dangerous Directors" *Financial Times* (16 December 1996).
9. Ball, G, "The Banned" *The Express* (4 June 1998).

Conclusion

Many SME owner-managers have never heard of the stage models of the OLC, so they will never voice the criticism that many small businesses move back and forth through the stages of development as trading conditions fluctuate, sometimes growing rapidly only to contract just as quickly as a battery of outside influences ebb and flow in their favour or otherwise. Most of our acquaintances are well aware of the external pressures that impact upon business performance and profitability and understand that they must adjust their business operations in line with external environmental conditions.

Conversely, the hidden elements of their own inner make-up, the neuroses and inner drives that 'make them tick' are not always understood as well. This is problematic in that the information they receive from stakeholders (both inside and outside the enterprise) are unconsciously filtered through cognitive processes that inform their decisions, attitudes, and so forth. Most perform this task without injury to the business itself. However, for some who display more extreme forms of neurotic behaviour in their managerial role, failure proneness can result. That this is unpleasant and psychologically damaging for those who bring it upon themselves is bad enough. For the innocent SMEs that have provided goods and services on credit, the impact can be equally devestating.

Generic models, whether they are concerned with growth, strategic planning or the myriad of other subjects we understand to be connected to management, have to be treated with caution. Such conceptual devices are rooted in the assumption that rationality prevails. This is not always the case. Human behaviour is interfaced between such conceptual devices and this is not always rational.

References

Argenti, J, *Corporate Collapse, The Causes and Symptoms* (London: McGraw Hill) 1976.

Ball, G, "The Banned" *The Express* (4 June 1998).

Beaver, G & P L Jennings, "Small Business Performance: A Management Perspective" Paper presented to the Small Business and Enterprise Development Conference, Leeds University (5-6 April 1995).

Berryman, J, "Small Business Failure and Bankruptcy: A Survey of the Literature" *European Small Business Journal* (1983) Vol.1, No. 4, pp. 47-59.

Birley, S & N Niktari, *The Failure of Owner-Managed Businesses: The Diagnosis of Accountants and Bankers* (London: Institute of Chartered Accountants) 1995.

Chell, E, "The Entrepreneurial Personality: A Few Ghosts Laid to Rest" *International Small Business Journal* (1985) Vol.3, No. 3, pp. 43-54.

Cohen, N, "Dangerous Directors" *Financial Times* (16 December 1996).

Churchill, N C & V L Lewis, "The Five Stages of Business Growth" *Harvard Business Review* (1983) Vol. 41, No .3, pp. 30-50.

Daft, R L, *Organisation Theory and Design* (St Paul: West) 5th edition, 1995.

Flamholz, E G, *How to Make the Transition from an Entrepreneurship to a Professionally Managed Firm* (San Francisco: Jossey-Bass) 1986.

Greiner, L E, "Evolution and Revolution as Organizations Grow" *Harvard Business Review* (1972) Vol. 50, No. 4, pp. 37-46.

Grinyer, H, D G Mayes & P McKiernan, *Sharpbenders: The Secrets of Unleashing Corporate Potential* (Oxford: Blackwell) 1988.

Haire, M, "Biological Models and Empirical Histories of the Growth of Organisations" in M Haire (ed.), *Modern Organisation Theory* (New York: John Wiley) 1959.

Handy, C, "The Age of Unreason" in J Henry (ed.), *Creative Management* (London: Sage) 1991.

Keasey, K & R Watson, "The Prediction of Small Company Failure: Some Behavioural Evidence for the UK" *Accounting and Business Research* (Winter 1991) Vol/ 22. No. 85, pp. 49-57.

Keasey, K & Watson, R, "The State of the Art of Small Firm Failure Prediction: Achievements and Prognosis" *International Small Business Journal* (1991) Vol. 9, No. 4, pp. 11-29.

Kets De Vries, M F R & D Miller, *The Neurotic Organization* (San Francisco: Jossey Bass) 1984.

McLelland, D C, *The Achieving Society* (Princeton: Van Nostrand) 1961.

Miller, D, "The Icarus Paradox" (1990) in C A Carnall (ed.), *Strategic Change* (Oxford: Butterworth Heinemann) 1997.

Miller, D, "The Architecture of Simplicity" *Academy of Management Review* (1993) Vol. 18, No. 1, pp. 116-138.

Miller, D & H Friesen, "A Longitudinal Study of the Corporate Life Cycle" *Management Science* (1984) Vol. 30, pp. 161-83.

Murphy, M, *Small Business Management* (London: Pitman) 1996.

Quinn, R E & K Cameron, "Organizational Life Cycles and Shifting Criteria of Effectiveness" *Management Science* (1983) Vol. 29, pp. 33-51.

Richardson, B, S Nwanko & S Richardson, "Understanding the Causes of Business Failure Crises: Generic Failure Types: Boiled Frogs, Drowned Frogs, Bullfrogs and Tadpoles" *Management Decision* (1994) Vol. 32, No. 4, pp. 9-22.

Rotter, J B, "Generalised Expectancies for Internal versus External Control of Reinforcement" *Psychological Monographs* (1966) Vol. 80, No. 609.

Smallbone, D, "Success and Failure in New Business Start-Ups" *International Small Business Journal* (1990) Vol. 8, No. 2, pp. 34-47.

Schumpeter, J A, *The Theory of Economic Development* (Cambridge, MA: Harvard University Press) 1934.

Scott, M & R Bruce, "Five Stages of Growth in Small Business" *Long Range Planning* (1987) Vol. 20, No. 3.

Steinmetz, L L, "Critical Stages of Small Business Growth: When they Occur and How to Survive them" *Business Horizons* (February 1969) pp. 29-36.

Urwick, L, "Problems of Growth in Industrial Undertakings" *BIM Proceedings* (1948) No. 2.

Villiers, C, "Boiled Frog Syndrome" *Management Today* (March 1989) pp.121-124.

Weitzel, W & E Jonsson, "Decline in Organisations: A Literature Integration and Extension" *Administrative Science Quarterly* (1989) Vol. 34, No. 1.

Chapter 5

BUSINESS PERFORMANCE AND VIABILITY

Terry Elliott

Introduction

One of the major distinguishing characteristics of the small to medium-sized enterprise (SME) is the limited resource base. Thus, a potentially viable business proposition may fail to flourish as expected because of a lack of recognition of resource limitations. It is essential that the SME is able to identify and manage the activities that are critical to their survival and growth.

Reasons for Business Failure

The reasons for failure in the small firm have attracted much attention. Hall (1995) provides three separate sets of explanations, which can be summarised as follows:

1. Small firms that survive over an extended period of time learn in detail how their costs are derived. Subsequently, they are able to develop efficient methods of cost control, which allows them to move along a 'critical growth path'.

   Differences in the size of firms represent different positions along this critical growth path for a given business sector. Firms that fail to understand their cost structures fully will not progress along the critical growth path. As a consequence, they will inevitably contract the products and services that are offered. If these fall below a specific threshold – the 'failure boundary' – the business will fail.

   Therefore, as the firm grows older, more is learnt of the true nature of costs and, more importantly, better accuracy is developed in estimating future cost trends. This acquired expertise enables the SME to avoid or pre-empt unpleasant surprises which would otherwise overwhelm the firm.

2. The second explanation identifies the small firm as represent-
ing 'limited portfolios' that are affected by the opportunities
open to them. These opportunities are made up of the products or services they offer and the markets in which they
operate – these can be regarded as a portfolio of assets.
However, these will be susceptible to economies of both scale
and scope.

Economies of scale is defined as the advantages to be
gained from size – typically, the opportunity to reduce unit
product cost by spreading what are essentially fixed costs
across a greater volume of output. Because of the intrinsic
size constraint that identifies the SME, there may be limited
opportunity for advance in this direction.

Economies of scope represent the advantages that can be
derived from offering combinations of products or from operating in particular combinations of markets. Examples of
economies of scope apply to organisations that are able to
transfer knowledge gained in one market into a completely
different sector. Thus, one could consider Canon's expertise
in camera lenses and its subsequent application to photocopiers as an example of this.

It becomes apparent that small firms will generally have
difficulty in dealing with larger organisations in these areas
and may have to develop alternative strategies in order to
compete and survive.

The 'limited portfolio' concept in relation to the SME can
be further developed in regard to the range of management
skills available. This is not to say that the level of managerial
talent will always be lower in the small firm. However, the
practical reality is that larger organisations are generally more
able to provide in-house training and sponsor attendance on
relevant management courses. This is likely to be part of a co-
ordinated staff development programme that has already
identified skills shortages and has allocated sufficient funds
for a training budget.

In summary, it can be noted that the more limited the range

and volume of managerial skills available to the firm, the more limited the range of situations its management team can exploit or confront. Hendry (1995) states that if a small firm is to grow, it needs to develop a management team with appropriate skills and knowledge to take it forward.

3. The third explanation given by Hall (1995) with regard to reasons for SME failure is related to the structure of markets (and segments of markets) they compete in. Basically, the number of firms that can successfully stay in business is related to the total size of the market. The danger for the small firm is when a segment in which they are operating becomes overcrowded with competition.

   This problem is likely to exist where barriers to entry are low – firms that see potential for profit and growth will move into these markets. An example given by Hall is that it does not take long to build up sufficient knowledge to become a house decorator as opposed to a lawyer. The failure rate within law firms tends to be lower than within the decorating business.

It is probable that all of the above explanations have some part to play in the failure of small firms. Hall (1995) also surveyed the owners of failed businesses, and their perceptions of the primary causes of failure fell into the following categories:

Internal operational issues:
- under-capitalisation;
- poor management of debt;
- inaccurate costing and estimating;
- poor management accounting.

External strategic issues:
- lack of demand;
- funding associated companies;

- reliance on a few customers;
- high interest rates;
- competitor behaviour;
- poor forecasting.

Personal issues:
- disagreement with partners.

Technological issues:
- inferior product/service.

Customer Requirements

The small firm needs to understand clearly the basis on which it is going to compete, and these must be oriented to the needs of their target customers. The challenge is then to determine that the operating processes are designed to deliver the desired outcomes at the minimum possible cost. This is achieved by developing 'performance objectives', which the firm needs to set itself, designed in such a way as to improve its overall competitiveness.

Slack (1995) identifies five broad performance objectives a firm should set itself in order to enhance its competitiveness by doing the following.

It should seek to develop:
1. A quality advantage by doing things right.
2. A flexibility advantage by varying or adapting what is done.
3. A reliability advantage by doing this consistently and on time.
4. A speed advantage by doing things quickly.
5. A cost advantage by doing things effectively and efficiently.

Peppard and Rowland (1995) identify a similar set of objectives which firms should use, as follows:
- quality;
- flexibility;

- delivery – speed and reliability;
- price;
- relationship management.

The quality objective can be explored in greater detail. Its two main aspects are consistency (how consistently the product or service conforms to specification) and capability (how well it meets the requirements of the customer).

Garvin (1984) has identified eight key dimensions of quality, as follows:

1. *Performance:* main operating characteristics of the product or service. For a car this could be top speed or fuel consumption.
2. *Features*: supplementary characteristics, e.g. colour, safety features.
3. *Reliability:* this is related to the dependability of the product or service.
4. *Conformance*: how closely the product or service conforms to specification.
5. *Durability:* how long a product can be used before it becomes too expensive to keep because of repairs or maintenance.
6. *Serviceability of the product:* can it be serviced easily and inexpensively.
7. *Aesthetics:* the style, feel, look of the product or service.
8. *Perceived quality:* the intangible aspects such as product, brand, company image.

Not all of the above dimensions can be applied to the service sector. Therefore, Fitzgerald *et al.* (1991) provide an alternative set that is more focussed on the needs of this sector.

- *Access:* the ease with which a customer can gain access to the service.
- *Aesthetics or appearance:* the way in which the point of service appears to the customer, e.g. the welcome and demeanour of staff or the décor.

- *Availability*: the availability of the service when required.
- *Cleanliness and tidiness.*
- *Comfort:* physical and mental comfort when experiencing the service, e.g. how comfortable the bank makes you feel when asking for an extension to borrowing facilities.
- *Competence:* the competency shown by the provider when delivering the service.
- *Communication:* the effectiveness of the communication between the provider and the customer. This could involve a range of communication approaches, both verbal and visual.
- *Courtesy*: the level of 'common courtesy' extended to customers when a service encounter takes place.
- *Friendliness:* this may mean different things across countries and cultures.
- *Reliability of the service.*
- *Responsiveness*: the level of responsiveness to customer requests, e.g. how quickly does an organisation respond to non-standard requests?
- *Security of the service*: e.g. is your money safe with your bank?

Understanding the Product and Service Delivery Process

Peppard and Rowland (1997) identified that all firms are built upon three broad pillars, which can be summarised as *people, technology* and *processes*. When designing processes to meet the market requirements and the customers within it, four key elements need to be considered:

- customer requirements;
- pattern of demand;
- constraints;
- efficiency targets.

These elements combine to set the deliverables for a product or services delivery process, known as the 'service task'

(Armistead, 1990). A clear understanding of this is critical if processes are to be redesigned to meet the needs of the firm and its customers.

At the interface between business operations and the end customer there is a growing awareness that value can be enhanced by delivering superior customer service quality. In the past some of the service sector (including public sector bodies) have defined value in terms of criteria established by professional employees that has not been tested out with reference to customers or clients. However, the concept of value will change over time as customer expectations are refined and as a result of competition. In seeking to enhance value, many organisations have focused on the development of service quality through customer care, which has been brought about by two key pressures.

The first of these is customer awareness of alternative products and providers of services. The second is changes in the business environment in relation to technology, legislation and the economy, e.g. deregulation of financial services or compulsory competitive tendering in local authorities.

Silvestro and Johnson (1990) carried out research into the UK service industry and identified fifteen dimensions of service quality that can be broadly categorised as:

- *'Hygiene factors'*: expected by the customer. Failure to deliver causes dissatisfaction.
- *'Enhancing factors'*: these lead to customer satisfaction but failure will not cause dissatisfaction.
- *'Dual threshold factors'*: where failure to deliver will cause dissatisfaction but delivery beyond a certain level will enhance customers' perception and lead to satisfaction.

In order to supply organisations such as Marks and Spencer, firms must meet very high standards of quality and reliability – these are the threshold or hygiene factors that are the basis for competition. These must be recognised by supplying firms and be the threshold level at which they perform. However, it may be wasteful in terms of time and money to go beyond these levels in order to win new customers.

The things that attract customers to buy from one company rather than another (assuming the hygiene factors are met by both) are called 'competitive edge' factors, and these will be different from the hygiene factors. These will also differ from one segment of the market to another – it is a question of understanding what is being bought, who is buying and why they are buying it.

Performance Management

Traditionally, successful business performance has been measured in terms of 'bottom line' profit that is then placed in an appropriate context, e.g. comparison with previous years' results or relevant business sector average. Return on capital employed or against net assets indicates the efficiency of the investment.

However, profit alone can be a very volatile measure. One has only to consider some of the more spectacular business failures of the recent past, such as Polly Peck (financial collapse) and Barings (unrecognised risk), and other businesses that have appeared to under-perform, such as IBM (lack of recognition of market changes). In recent years, Asda has been a good example of a firm that has been both one of the least profitable and also one of the most profitable in the retail sector. A key attribute of a successful company must therefore be to implement performance measures which, amongst other things, advise and guide executive decisions effectively.

'Tomorrow's Company' (RSA, 1995) reports that only five out of the eleven firms named as Britain's most profitable companies during the 1980s by *Management Today* have survived independently. Similarly, of the companies which made up the 'Fortune 500' in 1970, some two-thirds do not exist today. Thus, while profit is seen as a key measure of success and is still required, careful thought needs to be given to its most appropriate form and context.

Financial information alone will not help a company to evolve rapidly. In order to trigger successful improvement actions, information needs to focus on the causative factors of performance and, above all, assist predictions. Responsible business managers want to spot trouble in the early stages or seize opportunities ahead of the opposition. Better knowledge is required of how the company is performing across an entire series of dimensions.

As we have seen, traditional financial measures alone may be inadequate because they do not cover the broad balance of factors that influence and are affected by the company's activities. In addition, they fail to recognise the build-up of enterprise value or record its decline. In recent years there has been a growing consensus amongst professional commentators in this area that an information management system based solely on financial measures is not enough.

As Jack Welch of General Electric remarked: "The three most important things you need to measure in a business are customer satisfaction, employee satisfaction and cash flow." Others have developed this theme to widen the analysis with additional stakeholder groups such as suppliers and the local community, moving towards the arena of 'social accounting'. Interestingly, even well-respected gurus such as Tom Peters have revised their views on exactly what constitutes 'excellence' in an organisation. Thus, companies selected as being good performers, when measured against what seemed to be sensible criteria at the time, have not survived (Peters & Waterman, 1985). In retrospect, the prevailing criteria were inward-focused, giving less emphasis to customer and employee concerns than we would now expect.

This evolving vision is evidenced in a later work where Peters (1987) proclaims "the objective is not to be excellent because there is no place to stand anymore; the only excellent firms are those that are rapidly evolving". Others have examined the critical influence that an organisation's 'culture' can have on its economic performance. Kotter and Hesketh (1992) undertook a substantive study of the relationship between culture and performance and identified a 'performance-enhancing' culture as one that was strong, strategically appropriate and adaptive when outside forces changed.

One of the barriers to developing a performance-enhancing

culture is a firm's unrealistic perception of its own performance. A recent European benchmarking survey bears testimony to this tendency – while 40 per cent of UK manufacturing firms surveyed thought of themselves as 'world class' only 2.3 per cent of them were performing at a world class level!

To achieve consistent benefits, a business enterprise must install objective and predictive reporting systems within a culture that is focused on achieving continuous improvement. The challenge is to implement quality information systems, balance the change agenda, ensure customer focus and align teams to achieve process maturity. Kaplan and Norton (1996) argue that the next generation of business – 'Year 2000 companies' – will have management reporting and control systems that are fully integrated, with a common set of information entered once and accessible to all, supporting both internal and external reporting.

Data quality will be ensured via fully linked databases and systems. External financial reporting systems will have a two-way data exchange with integrated activity-based management systems, which will provide the necessary information to feed operational and strategic performance measurement systems.

One method of ensuring that attention is given to the critical strategic drivers of success is to form a broader set of performance measures into a 'balanced scorecard'. The scorecard technique recognises that companies need measures that view the organisation from a variety of standpoints including, for example, the needs of key stakeholders. In particular, more externally focused measures are required, as well as those covering the key area of organisational development for the future.

The scorecard provides the cornerstone of a strategic management system. Company managers are forced to clarify their thinking by reviewing the simultaneous impact of their actions from a number of perspectives – financial, customers, internal business processes and innovation and learning.

Case Study A

As past of its mission to supply high calibre facilities to students, staff and local residents, the University of Watermouth's Student Union had a print shop. In March 1996 it had four staff and the fixed assets that would have been found in a traditional printer, e.g. offset lithograph printing machines, a plate-making machine, a collating machine, photocopiers and, of more recent origin, Apple Mackintosh computers and laser printers for desktop publishing.

Sales had grown progressively and generated a healthy contribution, after costs, towards the overall Union finances. However, this was all to change. The four universities within the local conurbation agreed to cease printing their individual weekly and monthly newsletters and magazines and instead jointly produce a weekly student newspaper and a monthly magazine. As a result, the in-house production of Watermouth-specific weeklies and monthlies would cease and there would be a loss of revenue of the order of £16,000 per annum. As the Students' Union had a 'no redundancies' policy, the loss of such a large amount of revenue would drive the operation from profitability into loss and question the future survival of the firm.

A meeting of all concerned was held to discuss ways in which this challenge and potential threat to survival could be met. Issues of possible new business were discussed and the following conclusions drawn:

- *The printing market was expanding as businesses recognised the need to promote themselves.*

- *The expansion of the market was at the higher end, in the area of full-colour materials.*

- *There was a perceived shortfall in the consistency of quality offered by competitors to their customers.*

- *The expansion into the commercial market could be achieved by 'bolting on' a desktop publishing facility,* adding colour graphic design facilities that had not previously been offered.

• Since the merger with the nearby Riverside Technical college (now University College Riverside), there were now a considerable number of graphic design and fashion design students, most of whom compiled their very intricate work using Apple Mackintosh computers.

• Due to the free internet access given to students by universities, there were inherent problems within Academic Information Services (AIS) at Watermouth. Course tutors had previously insisted on final dissertations being submitted in a wordprocessed format. Expectations had now changed and nearly all modular coursework was expected in this format. This placed great strain on students who did not own a personal computer and printer for the following reasons:

a) gaining access to a computer within AIS was difficult because of the prevalence of 'web surfers';

b) once access to a computer was gained, files could be drawn from the central server to work on, but often could not be replaced in their enlarged state;

c) work which was completed and sent to print to the (monochrome) laser printers in AIS could often take up to three hours to print out. Should this work not be collected immediately following completion it was almost invariably creased by other students sifting through to retrieve their own work;

d) there were no colour printing facilities on campus;

It was agreed that the current level of equipment was obsolete, having been totally depreciated two years earlier. This was a situation that required urgent attention. Subsequently, both IBM and Apple Mackintosh computers, linked to a colour photocopier via a sever, were acquired. A customer survey was undertaken to identify needs and *any potential market gaps that could be exploited. Prices were increased to reflect the superior quality of the delivered product. As a result, turnover increased by 68 per cent for 'over the counter' transactions, not sufficient in itself to replace the lost revenue, but enough to recover the capital outlay in less than one year with the prospect of further growth in the future.*

An 'organisational health check' was undertaken to identify the key factors that determined the success of the business. These were specified and addressed in the following ways:

1) *Price of product/service had previously been discussed with customers at the time they used the service. A periodic review of competitors' prices was initiated.*

2) *Good relationship with suppliers is historic, as is the relationship with the closest competitors, the university.*

3) *Good relationship with customers, primarily the student body. A survey was undertaken to identify any 'perception gap' that may exist between the actual and perceived requirements.*

4) *Company brand/image. The firm redesigned its in-shop signage, internal advertisements in both the Fresher's and Student Union Handbooks and also external advertising.*

5) *Ability to respond quickly to customer requests had been difficult because of long-term sickness of a staff member, but was recognised as an issue that required urgent attention.*

6) *Ability to respond to market changes would be addressed by the expansion of computer facilities.*

7) *Capability to innovate would be addressed by professional team members, allowing for an interchange of knowledge and expertise.*

8) *Local contacts. It was recognised that there had been a weakness in this area in the past caused by a dependen-*

cy on in-house business. They had now started to build
a portfolio of external customers.
9) *Technological capability. Colour photocopying equipment was updated with a prospect of upgrade to digital
colour technology as soon as supplier availability per-
mitted.*
10)*Market share has been seen to grow as a high-quality
service was delivered to customers on a limited budget
at an affordable price.*

Measuring Business Probfitability

Whilst some organisations are able to quote prices for their products or services based on perceived costs plus a reasonable
mark-up, most businesses are competing against alternative suppliers of similar products or services. In these circumstances the
price charged may be critical if the order is to be won or customer interest maintained.

Where there is price constraint it is imperative that the business owner is fully aware of all the relevant costs that are being
incurred. To wait until the end of the financial year when the
auditor finally approves the accounts may be reckless – akin to
driving a car by looking in the rear-view mirror. Not only may
there be unexpected and nasty surprises because net profit is less
than anticipated (with the knock-on effect on planned expansion
or dividend payments), there may also be hidden forces at work.

For instance, a company that supplies a range of different
products or services may not be aware that the profits generated
by one are being diluted because another is effectively being
sold at a loss. This may not be apparent where some or all costs
are aggregated and the business, as a whole, is making a net
profit.

Thus, it is vital to have a clear ongoing vision of all costs as
they are incurred and to be able to accurately link them to each
product or service supplied by the business. It is important to
distinguish between the type of costs that tend to stay constant,

irrespective of the level of business activity and those that fluctuate because business goes up or down.

We classify the first group as *fixed* costs. They are often pre-
dictable to a fair degree of accuracy at the start of the financial
year. A good example would be business rates payable to the
local authority. If someone is employed on an annual agreed
salary, their wages are effectively a fixed cost as well.

The second group, by contrast, is only incurred as business
activity progresses and are classed as *variable* costs. Hence, in a
manufacturing business, raw materials incorporated into a product fall into this category, as would the wages of production-
related employees if paid on an hourly, flexible basis or on a
piece-rate.

Some costs inevitably fall into both classes, e.g. utility bills,
where a core standing charge is enhanced by the relevant usage
tariff. As a rule of thumb, each cost type should be addressed by
asking the question, "would this cost be reduced significantly if
we did less business?" Then classify the cost type accordingly.

Obviously, the price charged for a particular product or service should exceed the identified variable cost of its provision to
the customer – if this is not possible it questions the whole *raî-
son d'etre* of that particular part of the business. The difference
between the selling price and the cost of production or provision
is known as the *gross profit* because at this stage no account has
been taken of the fixed costs, which still have to be paid.

In essence, the entrepreneur gambles at the start of the year
that they will generate sufficient business to meet all of the
expected fixed costs. It is important to remember that the term
'gross profit' is something of a misnomer – if there is not sufficient funds to meet the fixed costs there will be a *net loss* at the
end of the year instead of a *net profit*.

It is better to view the business early in the year as generating
a *contribution* towards fixed costs rather than a gross profit.
When this contribution is equal to the fixed costs, this is known
as the *breakeven point* and indicates the level of business activity required to move into a profit situation. By comparing this
with the realistic maximum capacity (e.g. the number of working

hours in the year or productive capability), the *margin of safety* can be assessed.

Once the breakeven point has been reached, it is reasonable to quote for business based on the *marginal cost* of the next unit of activity (this is often the same as the variable cost, but may be distorted by suppliers' quantity discounts or overtime rates of pay).

Costs that can be attributed to an individual product or service are called *direct costs*; those which are shared are *indirect costs*. A system must be devised to allocate or charge these out to the product. It is the failure to adequately address this task that causes many business enterprises to inaccurately cost their products, leading to poor performance and loss of competitive edge.

Controlling Working Capital

To stay in business today and prosper in the future, the enterprise must be generating enough cash to pay the bills as they fall due. Unless there is sufficient cash available, it does not matter how 'profitable' the business is because the suppliers who are owed money (creditors) will not wait to be paid.

For an SME, shortage of ready cash to pay the bills leads to failure even if the business concept is commercially viable. Cash is the short-term necessity while profit is needed in the medium to long-term. It is vital to focus on cash first, profits second and finally growth. In practice, many owners focus on growth, then profits and finally cash, only to discover it is too late to save their business in the cash crisis that follows. This process of attempting to grow faster than available funding will allow is known as 'overtrading'.

'Cash' is the amount of money available right now to pay the bills. For any typical enterprise, cash is 'notes in the till' and money in the bank, including the amount of any agreed overdraft or loan that is as yet unused.

When considering the cash flow into and out of the business there are three key elements that can be controlled:

- *Debtors:* customers who still owe the firm money.

- *Stock*: materials, products in the process of being made and finished goods.

- *Creditors:* suppliers and others that the firm owes money to (including bank loans and overdrafts).

Debtors can be considered as the main flow of cash into the business and creditors as the main flow out. Stock represents the stage in between and needs to be kept to a workable minimum – obviously, products must be available to meet expected customer demand. This can be seen as a temporary store of business funds that needs to be converted into sales as quickly as possible.

There are other flows in and out, but these three must be controlled and used to the best advantage of the business. Together with cash balances they form the *working capital* of the business (also known as *net current assests*) and the process of control is known as *working capital management*.

The 'revolving door' nature of cash flow in and out of a business is known as the *operating cash cycle* and can be measured in practical terms as the time taken between initial commitment to purchase raw materials and the subsequent payment by customers for the firm's product that emerges from those raw materials. This theoretical maximum time cycle can be reduced to the extent that creditors can be persuaded to wait for their payment.

The overall aim in this financial juggling act is to ensure that the right amount of cash is in the right place at the right time. Too much in one place (such as stock) means too little elsewhere (such as exceeding the overdraft limit). Most businesses have to give credit to their customers (debtors) and hold stock which, taken together, would be more than they owe to suppliers. In this case there will always be a requirement for additional funding. There are three broad sources of extra funds – share issue or informal investment, retained profits from previous years' trading or borrowings (e.g. bank loan or overdraft).

If the business grows as planned, the operating cash cycle will expand and need more funds in roughly the same proportion. For example, a well-managed manufacturing business might need £250 extra funds for each extra £1,000 of turnover (a poorly managed one would need even more). On the same principle, reducing the size of the business or becoming more efficient will free up the cash that is in the working capital cycle.

The term 'net working assets' is the same as working capital without the cash element. It is determined by the following equation:

(stock + debtors) – amount owed to creditors = net working assests

The most important part of controlling working assets (and the most difficult) is to set realistic targets. The amounts of debtors and creditors and the level of stock will go up and down with your sales level, so targets need to be set as a percentage of sales. A target value in pounds can then be set that will fluctuate with sales.

One of the biggest headaches for the small business entrepreneur is ensuring that customers pay their bills on time. Several techniques can be employed to assist this task, which is commonly referred to as 'debtor control'. The starting point is usually to decide how often the firm will check the change in overall debtors. Normally this would be monthly, but individual debtors should be chased as soon as payment is overdue. Most companies have an awareness of what they expect 'target debtors' to be. This is the number of days of credit that they think it is reasonable for customers to take. In practice it has two components – the number of days of credit the standard terms of trade allow, plus the number of extra days the business is prepared to give, balancing the need for cash against the prevailing trends in the competitive marketplace.

Most businesses will analyse their total debtors position into what is known as an 'aged debtors list'. This breaks down, on a customer by customer basis, the amount owed and more importantly, how long it has been outstanding. As debts move into a pre-designated danger zone (for example, often three months or more), this will trigger action to retrieve the debt. One technique to encourage prompt payment is to offer a settlement discount for early payment – usually about 2 per cent of the total due. Alternatively, companies that do not feel they have sufficient in-house expertise in this area of credit control may choose to 'sell' their debts to an external agency that specialises in debt collection – a process known as factoring. This has the advantage of freeing up cash quickly, but comes at a price, thus eroding profit margins.

As mentioned above, in a competitive marketplace most firms will have a feel for the prevailing trends in their particular sector. Thus, there will be an industry average for relevant indicators of efficient business performance. This will show, for instance, the average time taken to turn stock around from purchase to sale, and similarly, the average periods for debtor turnover and creditor turnover. Obviously, the nature of the sector is crucial – thus, stock turnover in a perishable food retailer is much faster than a clothing retailer.

In maintaining the delicate balance of working capital management, there may be an understandable tendency to make suppliers wait a little longer for payment. However, there are sound business as well as ethical reasons for meeting payment deadlines. For a start, it provides an indication of sound financial health and will increase supplier confidence. This will probably lead to an enhanced relationship with the supplier, manifesting itself in improved delivery and service and the opportunity to increase the firm's credit rating in the future. Other preferential treatment may also ensue.

Case Study B

APEX is a well-established, family-owned business manufacturing textile items for industrial use. Its products are used in a variety of specialist markets, but one of the principal outlets is the laundry industry, particularly hospitals, nursing homes, etc. As part of the product range APEX has a copyright on a patented laundry bag. There are approximately 50 employees in what is essentially a cutting and sewing operation. Turnover is in excess of £1 million.

A SWOT analysis conducted last year identified a lack of

marketing skills as a 'weakness' and lack of sales demand as a 'threat'. Subsequent action to address these issues was successful, and as a result sales enquiries and actual orders increased significantly. Seven more sewing machinists were recruited to cope with the anticipated increase in output and by February 1998 the company was poised to take a quantum jump in performance, profit and cash flow.

In fact, the opposite happened. Although sales demand increased and continued to grow, the company does not appear to be generating more profit. Cash flow is poor, stock values have increased and the cost of poor quality has soared. Overtime has increased and orders must be rescheduled. All non-essential expenditure (such as staff training) has to be personally sanctioned by the Managing Director. Management response has varied from requesting investment for more process machinery and people to increase output, to proposals to make three administrative positions redundant in an effort to cut costs, to invoking disciplinary penalties for anyone who makes production errors that incur extra cost to the company.

A more detailed analysis identified the following situation:

- *The sales department is under constant pressure to achieve extra business orders so that a perceived level of necessary 'breakeven' activity can be maintained on a monthly basis.*
- *The production department is subsequently under pressure to respond to these orders and thus keep output in line with sales demand.*
- *Hence, there is a prevailing culture within the production area that everyone should be busy at all times.*
- *As a result, machines are being run flat out and people are rushing to get work out.*
- *This constant atmosphere of 'rush' leads to production errors and also means that there is no time for preventive maintenance on the machines.*

- *Inevitably, there is always a high level of work in progress (WIP), which increases the risk of quality problems and is a practical impediment to processing current orders efficiently.*
- *The financial consequences are that much of the firm's working capital is tied up in WIP, which affects cash flow, profitability and drives the perception of just how much activity is needed to achieve the elusive break-even target.*
- *The outcome of this is that there are many machine breakdowns, which disrupts the processing of orders and leads to customer dissatisfaction and the need to take retrieval action to make up lost time.*
- *This leads to constant high levels of overtime working and investment in extra 'insurance' machinery, both of which increase production costs and hence impact on breakeven targets once again.*
- *The long-term effects of working high levels of overtime are that concentration diminishes, leading to quality problems, disciplinary action, demoralisation and absenteeism.*

In summary, the company's productive capability is reduced, which impacts upon the level of sales that can be invoiced, costs are higher than expected, which directly affects profitability, and the credibility of the firm as a reliable supplier of quality products is tarnished in the eyes of its most important stakeholder – the customer.

This vicious circle was only broken when APEX was prepared to step back from the day to day treadmill of processing urgent orders and analyse the reasons for the persistent problems. This involved a painful process of realigning the company culture in order to dissipate the rushed atmosphere.

Essentially, there was a need to acknowledge that the varied nature of the production process inevitably meant that 'bottle-necks' would occur as work moved through the factory. In order to accommodate the constraints of the production flow, there would have to be an acceptance of the occasional need for 'idle time' in certain sections. There would also be a need for overall 'goal congruence' to ensure that the aggregate business targets of the whole firm were not being jeopardised by 'sub-optimisation' – for instance, achieving maximum productive potential for one subsection, even if the only visible outcome is a hefty contribution to the WIP mountain.

Even after the problem had been analysed and the benefits of moving from a vicious to a virtuous circle specified in financial and employee morale terms, there was still an intrinsic resistance to change, as the company culture was so firmly embedded.

Conclusion

There are a number of issues that need to be understood when developing relevant measures for small firms. Whilst keeping control of cash is essential for the small business, there are other aspects of business performance that need to be considered. The key point that needs to be remembered is that all business performance measures should monitor the factors that aim to differentiate the firm's products or services from those of its competitors.

These 'competitive edge' factors may be related to excellent product quality or producing a low cost product or service – the customer invariably wants both! Small firms need to identify the reasons why a customer would purchase their product or service constantly and build performance measures that monitor these areas.

References

Armistead, C G, "Service Operations and Strategy: Framework for Matching the Service Operations Task and the Service Delivery System" *International Journal of Service Industry Management* (1990) Vol. 1, No. 2.

Fitzgerald *et al.*, *Performance Measurement in Service Businesses* (CIMA) 1991.

Garvin, D A, "What does Product Quality Mean?" *Sloan Management Review* (Fall 1984).

Hall, G, *Surviving and Prospering in the Small Firm Sector* (London: Routledge) 1995.

Hendry, C *et al.*, *Strategy Through People: Adaptation and Learning in the SME* (London: Routledge) 1995.

Kaplan, R & D Norton, "Using the Balanced Scorecard as a Strategic Management System" *Harvard Business Review* (January-February 1996).

Kotter, J & J Hesketh, *Corporate Culture and Performance* (New York: Free Press) 1992.

Peppard, J & P Rowland, *The Essence of Business Re-engineering* (Hemel Hempstead: Prentice Hall) 1995.

Peters, T, *Thriving on Chaos* (Basingstoke: Macmillan) 1987.

Peters, T & R Waterman, *In Search of Excellence* (London: Harper and Row) 1982.

Royal Society of Arts, *Tomorrow's Company* (London) 1995.

Silvestro, R & R Johnson, *The Determinants of Service Quality – Hygiene and Enhancing Factors* (Warwick: Warwick University Business School) 1990.

Slack, N *et al., Operations Management* (London: Pitman) 1995.

Chapter 6

THE COMPETITIVE ENVIRONMENT

Tim Smith

Introduction

All businesses in the manufacturing or services sector, whether large or small, are operating in a complex and ever-changing environment. Because of the nature of the environment, it is impossible for any single organisation to control it. However, to accept this as a reason not to monitor it is to court disaster and place the business in the position of having continually to react to change without having any meaningful idea of where it is going or how it is going to get there.

This chapter aims to discuss some of the issues that confront the SME owner-manager when attempting to come to terms with the competitive environment in which they operate. For many entrepreneurs, the problem of assessing the environment in which they operate can seem to be such a daunting problem that the issue remains on the back burner whilst they get on with the 'real' or 'important' task of running the business on a day to day basis. As environmental change occurs at an alarmingly increasing rate, the size of the problem appears to grow at an even faster rate. What is to be done to confront this issue, given the limited resources that many small businesses can afford to devote to it?

In order to give meaning to any discussion of the competitive environment, the reasoning for monitoring it needs to be put in context. This chapter attempts to examine the issues from a marketing perspective and to view environmental analysis as an integral part of the organisation's planning process. In addition, consideration of the competitive environment needs to be viewed as a symptom of a firm's marketing orientation.

It becomes obvious that it is important to recognise clearly what we mean by such terms as 'marketing orientation' and 'environmental analysis'. It is also necessary to have an understanding of the benefits of planning, and the process that need to be followed in order to produce a meaningful plan that will help the organisation chart a course through the turbulent conditions in which they operate.

Developing a Market Orientation

Before attempting to discuss in any detail what market orientation is, it will be useful to clarify what marketing actually is, and perhaps more importantly, what it isn't.

According to McDonald (1995), "the central idea of marketing is of a matching between a company's capabilities and the wants and needs of customers in order to achieve the objectives of both parties". This is a useful way of defining what marketing is, as it gives the reader a working definition that can be applied to all organisations, regardless of their size, whether they are operating in consumer or industrial markets, whether they produce goods or services or operate in the profit or not-for-profit sectors of the economy. The definition also highlights the need to satisfy customers and gives this a meaningful context in that it appreciates that the ability to achieve this is not unlimited, but bound by the resources and capabilities of the organisation. Therefore, this definition of marketing is probably of greater use to the owner-manager than that given by The Chartered Institute of Marketing, which states that "marketing is the management process for identifying, anticipating, and satisfying customer requirements profitably".

Market orientation has been defined as having three major components: *customer orientation, competitor focus* and *interfunctional co-ordination* (Slater & Narver, 1994). From these three components we can see that two of them require the business to adopt an external focus to its activities, and the third necessitates that marketing is not to be viewed as something separate and distinct from all other areas of the businesses activities. At this point it is important to note that to strive for market orientation will require a serious commitment from the owner-manager that is communicated throughout the organisation. It will also involve the allocation of valuable resources, one of the most precious of which is time. There may also be financial costs that have to be taken into account. However, the firm that achieves this approach to doing business will be one that will be in a strong position to offer superior value to its customers, which lies at the heart of creating a sustainable competitive advantage

Customer Focus

Slater and Narver (1994) identify customer focus as being at the heart of market orientation. Having a customer focus means that an organisation has an in-depth knowledge of its customers' business. Their research has also identified that part of this customer focus involves spending considerable amounts of time with an organisation's customers, which allows them to constantly develop new ways of satisfying their needs. Continual measurement of customer commitment and satisfaction (and responding to what these measurements reveal) are vital to ensuring successful and long-term relationships. A customer-focused business must also realise that the relationship with customers is not only a job for the owner-manager or senior personnel, but the responsibility of all employees.

Competitor Focus

While still acknowledging the importance of focusing on the requirements of customers, it must not be forgotten that an in-depth awareness of the competition is also vital to a successful market-orientated approach to business. If business can be likened to a game of chess, the successful player will be the one that has paid close attention to their opponent and successfully attempts to consider what moves they may be able to make, both in the short and long-term. Again, to monitor the competition successfully requires a co-ordinated effort from all areas of the business, and relevant information needs to be communicated to those whom it may concern. For example, information concerning the development of a new product or service by a competitor may be picked up by a salesperson and reported to the sales and/or marketing function, but to be of value this information may need to be shared with those responsible for R&D. There is little point in collecting and storing information for its own sake.

Interfunctional Co-ordination

Interfunctonal co-ordination involves all personnel and other resources to be working together in an attempt to create superior value for their customers. This is based on the premise that everyone in the firm needs to realise their ability to help create and maintain a sustainable competitive advantage. This is usually more true for small and medium-sized enterprises than larger organisations, and in theory should be easier for them to achieve because of the fewer individuals who need to communicate with each other. Nevertheless, many owner-managers often feel the need to keep company information to themselves and often fail to achieve co-ordination and employee commitment, despite their relatively small size.

If an organisation has traditionally adopted an internal rather than an external approach to business (see discussion of product orientation below), then a conscious decision needs to be taken to change. Wherever the source of this desire to change the focus comes from, there is a very limited chance of success unless the commitment of the owner-manager can be gained. This writer's experience has been that the change of focus is often only learnt after an unpleasant experience, or the business has reached a point where there has come a realisation that 'perhaps things need to be done differently'.

This outlook is very different to that which is apparent in many businesses, regardless of size or sphere of operations. Too many organisations do not have this external focus and can be seen to be practicing one of the following concepts:

- the production concept;
- the product concept;
- the selling concept (source: Kotler 1996).

The *production concept* is based on the idea that the key to achieving success in business lies in providing customers with products or services that are as widely available and affordable as possible. This leads to the business striving to achieve the greatest possible efficiencies in production and distribution, and may lead to success in certain circumstances, e.g. where demand for a product exceeds the supply of it. However, this is a rare occurrence and an approach that does not pay close attention to the wants and needs of customers. Suffice to say that the classic example of a successful practitioner of this concept was the father of mass production, Henry Ford.

The *product concept* is based on the premise that customers will tend to favour those products that possess the highest attributes of quality, performance and features. Whilst the importance of these is not to be called into question, it is possible that producers can fall in love with their products and lose sight of the market, which may or may not exist for it. Everybody remembers the failure of the 'Sinclair C5' in the 1980s, even though the product could be said to have been a form of economic and environmentally friendly transport. It is not only the C5 that has failed to achieve success in the marketplace. The harsh reality is that the vast majority of new products that are launched into the marketplace fail, thus, no matter how good you believe your product or service to be, potential customers may feel otherwise.

The *selling concept* is based around the belief that businesses need to overcome an inherent unwillingness in the minds of customers to purchase their products. It is therefore the job of the organisation to maintain a sustained selling effort to overcome this barrier. The problem with this idea is that it tends to concentrate on the needs of the seller rather than those of the purchaser. If a customer is persuaded to buy a product that they do not really want or need or does not live up to the claims of the seller, then dissatisfaction occurs. This can lead to the deterioration of a relationship with a valued customer or inhibit the development of a potentially longer term and profitable relationship with new customers.

Having identified marketing as a concept (or orientation), it is important to differentiate it from marketing as a function within the organisation. Briefly, the marketing function may be seen as the management of the 'marketing mix' (product, price, place and promotion). These are the tools the marketer has to work with in order to implement the marketing concept or to achieve a marketing orientation for the organisation. Many companies undertake what may be described as 'marketing activities', such as spending money promoting their goods and services or developing new products. However, unless these activities occur as part of a co-ordinated effort within the organisation and are driven by the desire to satisfy customer wants and needs, the company cannot be seen as being market-orientated.

Case Study A

Some years ago, a small, local engineering company approached me to 'do a consultancy' project for them. A meeting was arranged with the owner-manager, who felt that he needed some help with marketing. The project turned out to be 'finding a market' for three new products that he had developed. The products had been well designed and samples produced that met and exceeded all the different tests that were necessary for them to undergo. Unfortunately for the owner-manager, the research that was subsequently undertaken identified that changes had occurred in the marketplace that had made his products obsolete. Understandably, the client felt disappointed with the result, especially as it had cost him a considerable amount of money. It was pointed out to him that perhaps he had approached the whole idea from the wrong angle, and had he looked for a market before producing the product he would have saved himself a considerable amount of time, effort and money. To give him his due credit he was heard to relate his experience at a gathering of small businessmen and had the grace to admit that he had learned a very valuable lesson.

To summarise, a market orientation requires the organisation to move from being purely internally focused to adopting an external focus. This does not mean that the organisation can afford to ignore what occurs internally, but rather, sees this in the context of a dynamic operating environment. The issue for the owner-manger becomes one of how to match the limited resources of the firm with the identified needs of customers within the constraints of the largely uncontrollable forces in the external environment. Therefore, we now need to begin to identify the forces, both internal and external, that need to be taken into account.

The Marketing Planning Process

Before moving on to discuss the marketing environment, it is important to discuss the process of marketing planning, which itself necessitates an examination of the marketing environment. Essentially, marketing planning is a matching process between customer needs and wants and the firm's resources and capabilities within an ever-changing external environment. For practical purposes, the process can be broken down into three components:

- *Phase 1*: Setting the organisational goals in terms of mission and corporate objectives.

- *Phase 2*: Carrying out a marketing audit of the company's external and internal environment.

- *Phase 3*: Formulating marketing objectives and strategies. Objectives need to be SMART.

  Specific about what is to be achieved.

  Measurable so that there can be confirmation of whether or not they are achieved.

  Agreed with those responsible for achieving them.

  Realistic so that they can be achieve.

  Timebound with a date set for achievement.

From this McDonald (1995) goes on to identify the contents of a marketing plan as:

- mission or purpose statement;
- summary of past years' performance;
- summary of financial projections;
- a market overview;
- SWOT analysis of major products/markets/segments;
- portfolio summary;
- major assumptions;
- marketing objectives and strategies for the next three years;
- financial projections for the next three years;
- detailed one year operational plan, with forecasts and budgets.

At the outset it is important to notice that the process begins with the firm's mission and corporate objectives. The marketing plan needs to be working toward the same goals as the overall plan for the business. However, corporate objectives may be expressed in quantitative terms, such as a target for return on capital employed, whereas marketing plans will usually contain objectives that incorporate qualitative aspects, such as relating to issues of customer service or market segments to be targeted. When attempting to produce a marketing plan, too many owner-managers attempt to start the process with phase three of the process. This can lead to a business that is operating on the 'ready, fire, aim' principle. Whilst many SMEs do manage to survive on this principle and develop qualities such as being able to respond or react quickly, it can often lead to the business going in the wrong direction or missing other opportunities that may be more attractive and profitable.

This is why it is important to spend time addressing the areas identified in phase two of the process. Through the process of the marketing audit, SWOT analysis and the resultant assumptions about the future operating environment, more realistic objectives and strategies can be developed. Even if assumptions made prove to be less than 100 per cent accurate there are still valid reasons for undergoing this process, as it is indicative of a firm that is starting to take a strategic, longer term view of its business rather than the shorter term, more operational view.

Case Study B

Arthur Brown established his business with his partner Geoff in 1986. By the early-1990s the business had grown and employed some 25 people. Profitability was good and Arthur had achieved his long-standing ambition of owning a Jaguar. However, there were problems. Arthur wanted the business to grow, but he was finding that he spent a very large proportion of his time sorting out problems on the shop floor and responding to customer queries. With help from a local business school, Arthur began to adopt a more long-term approach to his business. With his management team he began the process of developing a marketing plan. The process was met with some resistance at first, but eventually the plan was written and its implementation began. Apart from the obvious benefit of having clearly defined objectives and strategies for his business, Arthur found more time in planning for the future. One of the key benefits for him was that the plan had identified and clarified many issues that the business had to face. The process of marketing planning had been a catalyst in improving communications with employees, leading to a greater understanding of their roles and responsibilities in the organisation. Arthur has now managed "to let people get on with the jobs that they're supposed to do, without bothering me all the time". He now feels that he has more time to spend on dealing with 'the bigger issues'.

The Marketing Environment for SMEs

Any business that is aiming to be successful in terms of survival and growth needs to work towards an understanding of where that business stands in relation to the bigger picture. As Peter Drucker stated, "business does not operate in a vacuum". Any firm that intends to plan for the future needs to answer three basic questions:

1. Where are we now?
2. Where do we want to get to?
3. How are we going to get there?

In order to answer the first question, the firm must examine the environment it is operating in. (Issues relating to the other two questions will be dealt with below.)

For all businesses, regardless of size, there is nothing more important than the future. It would therefore seem logical that firms dedicate time and resources to a consideration of it. If these resources are committed to a consideration of the future, then there must be an acceptance that the future is going to necessitate a favourable attitude to change. Even if the firm's view of their future is never going to be completely accurate, a culture that accepts change will help that organisation to respond to unforeseen changes. It is with this mindset that we can begin to examine how SMEs can begin to benefit from environmental analysis.

Kotler (1991) sees the marketing environment as being "made up of the actors and forces that affect the company's ability to develop and maintain successful transactions and relationships with its target customers".

The marketing environment is usually discussed under two separate headings: the microenvironment and the macroenvironment. The microenvironment may be seen as consisting of elements that the firm interacts with in an immediate sense and may include the company, customers, competitors, suppliers, the public and sources of finances. The macroenvironment is far broader than the microenvironment and consists of forces that are largely beyond the control of the firm, regardless of its size. The major factors to be taken into account are covered by the acronym PEST (Political, Economic, Socio/Cultural and Technological). This is not an exhaustive list and each element mentioned might be further subdivided to give the firm a clearer idea of what elements are likely to have an effect on their operation. Brassington and Pettitt (1997) provide a useful breakdown, which includes many of the factors in the external environment that will have some greater or lesser effect on most firms regardless of whether they are large or small, produce products or provide a service, whether trade in domestic and/or overseas markets. Under the PEST heading they identify the following areas that need to be monitored.

1. Political/legal
- the EU;
- national government;
- local government;
- regulatory bodies;
- trade associations.

2. Economic/competitive
- market structure;
- government policy;
- trading blocs;
- taxation;
- interest rates.

3. Sociocultural
- demographics;
- culture;
- attitudes and current issues.

4. Technological innovation affecting
- products;
- materials/components;
- processes;
- distribution;
- marketing/administration.

Monitoring the external environment must be an essential activity for any firm that lays any claim to market orientation. Before any action can be taken by a business, it is imperative that the organisation looks outside itself. By doing this there should be a growing realisation of the effect that external factors have on such issues as identifying customer needs and pricing policies, as well as the management of all the major components of the marketing mix (product, price, place and promotion).

The process of monitoring and assessing the impact of the external environment is known as *environmental scanning*. This process, whether carried out formally or informally, is of vital importance but is also complex, time consuming and expensive. Even the best firms cannot hope to develop the perfect system, owing to the complexity and diversity of the ever-changing world in which they operate. It is this complexity and dynamic nature of the environment that is often cited by SMEs as a valid reason for not even attempting to monitor it, or indeed, to proceed with the process of marketing planning.

How can the SME come to terms with this problem? It has to be acknowledged at the outset that it is not a simple task, and that if monitoring the current environment is problematic, trying to make assumptions about the future will never be 100 per cent accurate. Secondly, it needs to be recognised that there must be a person in the firm who has responsibility for the process. Often this may be the owner-manager or some senior person in the organisation. Whoever has the responsibility needs to have a commitment to their task and the support of colleagues. It must also be accepted that the collection of information in itself is not sufficient. Information needs to be processed, analysed and then distributed to relevant members of the organisation so that conclusions can be drawn from it and thus provide a basis for future action.

The most important thing for the SME to achieve by monitoring the environment is the identification of the key issues that affect its performance and ability to survive in the longer term. Learning to ask the right questions is the first step towards finding the right answers. For many owner-managers, time spent on this stage of the process will help to avoid the problem of information overload later on, which may lead to discouragement and ultimately to the abandonment of the process. Not only will the identification of the right factors lead to environmental scanning becoming a job of manageable proportions, it will enable it to become an ongoing process. There is little point in seeing scanning as a 'one-off' task when it is clear that change is perhaps the only certainty in the environment.

Johnson and Scholes (1993) advocate a six stage approach to environmental analysis (adapted by Fifield and Gilligan (1997)) that may be useful in not only assessing the current state of the environment, but also in helping the firm to look to the future. The stages are as follows.

Stage 1	Audit the environment to identify the factors that have influenced the organisation's development and previous performance, the probable direction in which the environment will develop and the likely key influences.
Stage 2	Assess the nature of the environment and the source of any uncertainty that is likely to exist.
Stage 3	Examine specific environmental factors, including the nature of each market sector the organisation operates in.
Stage 4	Analyse the firm's strategic position by means of strategic group analysis and market share analysis.
Stage 5	Identify in detail how environmental forces will affect the organisation and the types of opportunities and threats that will emerge.

Stage 6	In the light of stages 1-5, decide upon the future ideal strategic position and determine the implications for strategies, structures and systems.

Regarding stage five (market share analysis), it needs to be acknowledged that for many SMEs, market share is either of very little relevance or almost impossible to calculate. Therefore, it is important to attempt to identify a criterion that does have meaning in relation to markets served and competitors' actions.

Another framework that may be usefully applied by the SME is Michael Porter's 'five forces model'(1990). Porter identifies five major competitive forces that determine industry profitability. These are:

1. *Industry competitors:* i.e. the rivalry that already exits between firms.
2. *Potential entrants:* i.e. the threat of new competitors entering the industry
3. *Substitutes:* i.e. the threat posed by substitute products or services.
4. *Suppliers:* i.e. the bargaining power of suppliers (for SMEs this will often relate to the issue of many suppliers being larger companies than they are).
5. *Buyers:* i.e. the bargaining power of buyers (for many SMEs customers will be larger companies who often expect suppliers to provide very favourable terms in relation to price, delivery, service, etc.).

Having identified the key environmental factors to monitor, the firm is now in a position to draw conclusions from examining factors they have some control over. These are usually internal and relate to elements of the marketing mix, whereas those that may be regarded as uncontrollable are usually external. The firm is now at a point where it can begin to answer the first question posed earlier in this chapter – where are we now? Being able to answer this deceptively simple question is fundamental to developing realistic marketing objectives and the strategies needed to achieve them.

Approaches to Planning for the Owner-Manager

Thus far, environmental analysis has been discussed within the context of a formal planning system, yet it is important to acknowledge that planning may be formal or informal. Hannon and Thereon (1998) state that:

> *...there is an ongoing debate within the academic literature about the value of the business plan within the small firm. On closer inspection of the research, there appears to be clear benefits in the use of business planning as a process within the smaller business. This is in contrast to the production of a business plan as an output.*

They go on to draw several conclusions from their research on planning and strategic awareness in small firms, which have important managerial and policy implications, as listed below.

- Business planning, as a process, appears to be a more valuable small business tool than the production of a business plan. The planning process need not be formal.
- Whether formal or informal, effective business planning is a rigorous process that challenges existing preconceptions.
- Business and support organisations' perceptions of the value and use of business plans appear to be quite different.
- Understanding the environment within which the small business operates, and how to respond to it, is critical to both the business planning process and the management of the small firm.
- Small businesses with different levels of strategic awareness capability and effectiveness have different characteristics and needs.

Whilst these findings may be music to the ears of some owner-managers, they do not provide an excuse for passing off a lack of planning in their business as "an informal system". Hannon and Atherton's research would also seem to highlight that there is never going to be one single approach to planning that can be applied to all SMEs. They also accept the fact that many owner-managers are not "professional managers", and as such are not formalised managers. If we accept this then perhaps we can begin to develop an argument that favours the adoption of, or at least the reference to a formal planning model that may ensure that the owner-manager has some form of guidance through the complex process of planning. This idea does not mean that the planner becomes a slave to a model that may be inappropriate. Experience has shown that owner-managers do not blindly accept models or frameworks without question. Many owner-managers display an ability to modify ideas presented by academics to suit their own specific situation and particular needs.

Implementing and Controlling the Plan

Implementation

Whatever approach to planning is adopted by the SME, it needs to be remembered that the production of a plan in itself is not the answer to achieving success in business. From the marketing planning model outlined above, it can be seen that a plan needs to be capable of being implemented. This presupposes that the plan is grounded in reality rather than being something akin to a wish list that the owner-manager would like to achieve. In order to achieve this, it is important that the plan is not compiled without reference to the people in the organisation who will be carrying it out.

Many writers identify one of the main requirements for successful implementation to be effective communication within the firm. The communication process needs to begin from the time that the idea of planning first arises, and is essential through all the stages of the process. Some owner-managers find this difficult. This difficulty often arises from the fact that that the business is their 'baby' and they know what is best for it. In practice, however, involvement from employees at all levels can often provide insights that are not possible from the lofty tower of the owner-manager's office. Involving employees can also be a valuable method of gaining their commitment to the plan and providing them with a sense of motivation because they know in which direction the firm is heading. Plans should provide explicit statements of what needs to be done and who is responsible for doing it.

Control

Controlling the plan helps to ensure that desired results are achieved. Fifield and Gilligan (1997) state that control systems are a matter of balancing four primary issues:

* standard setting;
* performance measurement;
* performance diagnosis;
* taking corrective action (if required).

Standard setting occurs in the earlier phases of the planning process. Therefore, it is critical that objectives are expressed in such a way that can be measured. Setting objectives, such as 'growth', without specifying the rate, the time period for achievement and consideration of where that growth is going to come from leads to a plan that will be difficult to control and ultimately cease to be viewed as an important working document within the firm.

Performance measurement is concerned with measuring what was achieved against what should have been achieved. Measurement is ususally broken down to cover areas of quantity, quality and cost. These areas can be analysed in relation to the operational areas of the firm, i.e. sales analysis, market analysis, human resource analysis, physical resource and financial analysis.

In order for control systems to be effective they need to measure key aspects of the above at meaningful intervals. Identifying a problem when it is too late to take corrective action is an admission that your system is at fault. The key to successful control of the plan lies in the identification of key performance indicators that can be measured with the minimum of time and effort. Research has shown that those firms that are the most successful at controlling their plans are the ones that have fewer rather than more performance indicators.

Controlling the plan demonstrates that the process of planning is a continuous one, not merely a one-off event. It also ensures that the firm maintains an external focus. Because it is impossible to predict the future with 100 per cent accuracy in dynamic operating environments, the control process should foster flexibility within the firm. It also has to be remembered that the planner can get things wrong. If this is so, then it is important that the plan is changed. Plans are written on paper and not carved in stone. Unforeseen changes do occur and it is better to make changes before problems occur than blindly follow a course of action merely because "it's in the plan".

There is no one system of control that is right for every firm. To ensure that effective control takes place will depend on the identification of key indicators for a particular firm operating in their specific environment.

Conclusion

Analysis of the environment is a key part of the planning process for all businesses, regardless of size. The complexity of the task will depend on the type of business and its operating environment. Planning requires the organisation to adopt an external focus and can be seen as an important step towards the development of a market orientation. The process of putting a plan together needs to be seen as being at least as important as the resultant plan. Also, planning that is effective will be seen as a continuous process within the firm. When producing a plan it is vital to remember that the plan needs to be capable of being carried out and controlled.

Many writers have detailed the benefits and pitfalls of planning. They tend to focus on the following issues.

Benefits of (Effective) Marketing Planning

1. Improved communication and motivation in the firm

Because the process of planning requires the firm to consider where it intends to go the owner-manager and the employees of the firm should be able to see where they are heading. The planning process can also indicate that the firm does see itself as having a future. Effective planning will be an inclusive rather than exclusive process, and will take into account the views and opinions of a wide range of employees.

2. High levels of actionable market information

The process of marketing planning requires the firm to collect and analyse information about the market, competitors and the environment. Done well, this should help lead to the establishment of a market information system that can regularly be updated and help minimise the risk of making poor decisions.

3. Greater interfunctional co-ordination

For a plan to be of use to a firm, the people involved in its operationalisation need to realise that the activities of one area of the business will have an effect on others. For example, the marketing function cannot exist and operate independently of finance or production. Even in very small businesses, employees can often regard themselves as working in isolation from other functional areas.

4. Accepting the need for continuous change

Any examination of the factors affecting a business will highlight that change is a fact of life. Attempting to ignore change will ultimately lead to problems for a business. Although many changes that occur will be beyond the control of the SME, it must surely be accepted that it is better to see changes coming before they arrive so the firm can plan for them.

Problems Encountered in Marketing Planning

Despite these obvious benefits it needs to be remembered that problems can occur in attempting to develop a plan, and that a plan in itself is not a magic wand guaranteeing business success. Below are some of the problems that a firm may encounter.

1. **The lack of a plan for planning**

   A plan cannot be put together without thinking about *how* it will be put together. Whoever has the responsibility for planning needs to consider a number of issues. What skills and resources will the development of a plan require? Does the firm possess these skills, and if not, how can they be acquired? Will there be support for planning within the firm?

2. **Confusion over planning terms**

   Do employees who will be involved in the process all understand the language of planning? Confusion can often occur when one person's understanding of terminology is different to others'.

3. **Too much detail too far ahead**

   As discussed earlier, environments are changing at an ever-increasing rate. Thus, it is unwise to try and plan too far into the future. Whilst it is laudable to adopt a strategic perspective, it needs to be realised that beyond a certain time in the future it is unrealistic to try and produce strategies in too much detail. How far into the future one may realistically plan will depend on the specific situation of each business in relation to the external factors that affect it.

4. **Planning as a ritual**

   Although this point has been made above it is worth mentioning again. Planning is a continuous process that does not end with the production of the plan itself. Plans that are produced in this way tend to finish up unread and unused on a shelf in some remote place in the firm.

5. **The delegation of planning to a planner**

   If the plan is put together by the owner-manager without reference to other members of the organisation, an opportunity to produce a valuable asset to the company will have been missed. Far from being a motivating factor in the business, there is a strong probability that employees will view the plan with suspicion. It is also very difficult for one person to be able to produce a realistic plan that takes into account all relevant factors from both within and outside the business.

6. **Too little too late**

   Although a marketing plan can be of great use to the business there are limits to what it can help achieve. There are many examples of planning being seen as a need too late in the day. Planning cannot reverse years of decline when the receivers are knocking at the door of the office. It is far better to plan before this situation is even a possibility.

The marketing plan and the process that produces it can never be a guarantee of success. However, if done well it should help the business reach a greater understanding of where it stands and where the best direction may be for it to proceed in an uncertain and ever-changing world.

References

Aaker, D A, *Strategic Market Management* (New York: Wiley) 4th edition, 1995.

Brassington, F & S Pettitt, *Principles of Marketing* (London: Pitman Publishing) 1997.

Fifield, P, *Marketing Strategy* (London: Butterworth Heinemann) 2nd edition, 1998.

Fifield, P & C Gilligan, *Strategic Marketing Management 1997/1998* (London: Butterworth Heinemann) 1998.

Hannon, P D & A Atherton, "Small Firm Success and the Art of Orienteering: The Value of Plans, Planning and Strategic Awareness in the Competitive Small Firm" *Journal of Small Business and Enterprise Development* (1998) Vol. 5, No. 2.

Johnson, G & K Scholes, *Exploring Corporate Strategy* (London: Prentice Hall) 3rd edition, 1993.

Kotler, P, G Armstrong, J Saunders & V Wong, *Principles of Marketing* (London: Prentice Hall) European edition, 1996.

Littler, D & D Wilson, *Marketing Strategy* (London: Butterworth Heinemann) 1995.

McDonald, M, *Marketing Plans: How to Prepare Them, How to Use Them* (London: Heinemann Butterworth) 3rd edition, 1995.

Piercy, N, *Market-Led Strategic Change* (London: Butterworth Heinemann) 2nd edition, 1997.

Porter, M E, "How Competitive Forces Shape Strategy" *Harvard Business Review* (1979) Vol. 57, No.2.

Porter, M E, *Competitive Strategy* (New York: Free Press) 1980.

Slater, S F & J C Narver, "Market Orientation, Customer Value, and Superior Performance" *Business Horizons* (March-April 1994).

Walker Jr, O C, W H Boyd Jr & J C Larreche, *Marketing Strategy: Planning and Implementation* (Boston: Irwin) 1992.

Wilson, R M S & C Gilligan, *Strategic Marketing Management, Planning Implementation and Control* (London: Heinemann Butterworth) 2nd edition, 1997.

Chapter 7

LEADERSHIP AND STRATEGY CHALLENGES

David MacGregor

Introduction

This chapter examines the process of strategic management in the SME context. SME owner-managers' strategies are rarely recorded or communicated and are often not subject to the analytical or critically evaluatory frameworks that identify the strategic management process in the corporate sector. This chapter seeks to outline a dynamic and innovation-oriented approach to understanding the process of strategy development, choice, evaluation and implementation within the SME and to highlight the uniqueness found in SMEs.

Much is made in management texts of the hierarchies and structures of larger organisations, but the emphasis on the structural appears to be sadly neglected in the SME literature. This might be because of the inherited structures of family or "buy-out" SMEs, or because SMEs grow organically and, often by default, chaotically. Yet it is in this chaos that uniqueness and contra-distinctiveness may be found. This chapter seeks to examine and develop these themes.

One of the aims of the study of strategic management in the SME sector is to contextualise and give authenticity to the 'strategic' experiences of entrepreneurs. Much of the literature in this field is either of the 'how to' technical manual type or written in a theoretical academic style. This chapter attempts a reconciliation of the two. The developmental or innovative aspects of this chapter encompass materials drawn from empirical work conducted with SME owner-managers through Bolton Business School's Centre for Enterprise and Management.

The Nature of Strategic Management

Strategic management is largely regarded as the rational process by which senior management identifies courses of action and responses to complex and dynamic environmental forces. It is traditionally concerned with hegemony, size, the utilisation of resources, achieving dominant positions and internalising issues of control and fit. The scale, scope and complexity of the strategic management field are problematic in that there is no overarching, generic core body of knowledge. There are instead contextual understandings of what is 'strategic' and a range of competing and exclusive schools of thought. This difficulty of definition prevents any conclusive diagnosis of the effectiveness of strategic management as an aid to organisational effectiveness, yet the methodological and theoretical difficulties with the field (McKiernan & Morris, 1994) enable invention and reinvention of contextual understanding of what is 'strategic'. This is particularly useful in the SME sector where there is both scope for reinvention of the strategy process to suit the context and an urgent need to develop new and even contra-distinctive understandings of the strategy process that are directly applicable to the SME sector.

The early fundamentals of strategic management are largely drawn from Industrial Organisation (IO) theory (Caves, 1980; Porter, 1980). There is a central methodological problem with IO strategic management in 'that the lack of a clear causal link between strategic intent, articulated strategy, realised strategic action and implementation causes discontinuities in the process. The behavioural aspects of the strategy process and the complex motivations of the actors are often written out of the IO theory literature in favour of economic rationality and the need to create competitive advantage and profitability through industry positioning.

Strategic management has some underpinning certainties. It is largely a process that requires broad overviews of the internal and external strategic variables. Much of the literature in the strategic management field roughly divides into two distinct schools of thought: the IO view outlined above and the resource-based view. The resource-based approach tends to place greater emphasis on the firm's internal resources, competencies and capabilities as the sources of competitive advantage. This approach internalises the strategic processes and enables the entrepreneur/owner-manager to have more discretion over the strategic variables to be considered and developed. It is often useful to measure and understand the causal relationships between business start-up, cash utilisation and the resource base of the organisation as a measure of both organisational effectiveness and efficiency. Added to this are the dual problems of stakeholder expectations (most notably the bank) and the problems of identifying the ratio of tangible against intangible resources on the balance sheet.

Whilst it is difficult to make generalisations about the preferred strategy-making style of SME owner-managers and entrepreneurs, the greater discretion afforded under the resource-based view and the difficulties inherent in positioning within globalised industry structures found in IO theory mean that many entrepreneurs tend to focus upon that which is 'closest to home'.

The key elements of the resource based view in the SME context can be summarised as follows.

Competencies

These are activities the organisation can do well, often referred to as 'core' competencies. It is basically what staff in the organisation can do to make profit or create competitive advantage. Later in this chapter we will consider the product or service task, and the competencies are what develops and enhances the product or service task for customers. These competencies may be design, testing, manufacture, distribution, marketing, retailing or after-care service.

Capabilities

Capabilities are collections of competencies that are linked together systematically and synergistically to provide strategic outcomes, competitive advantage or superior profitability. The capabilities of organisations in particular SMEs are often collections of competencies that are congregated around a skill or task. This skill or task usually emanates from the entrepreneur's concept of the 'right' core competence and is 'passed on' to other staff who replicate the process, often with less enthusiasm than the entrepreneur. This builds capabilities, the multiples of which lead to enhanced profitability and growth.

Other capabilities are bolted on to the organisation as and when required. Functional area such as accounting, legal services or health and safety, do not become part of the organisation's strategic capabilities until there is a need for them to do so. The main motivation for SMEs to develop additional 'non-core' capabilities is usually compliance or congruence with industry norms, or in other words, it is expected of them.

Resources

These are those tangible (and increasingly intangible) aspects of the organisation's infrastructure that underpin and support the competencies and capabilities. Issues of resources for growing small businesses are crucial; too little and the business is starved of the cash and assets required to sustain its early development, too much and the business grows its infastructure too quickly and collapses under its own inertia.

Strategic management, particularly from a resource-based standpoint, can be seen as an holistic conceptual field in that it is concerned with the whole organisation. It is also significant in that it uses theories and ideas drawn from areas as diverse as financial management, economics and organisational behaviour. Previously familiar areas of experience and expertise are often incorporated into the strategic process, although many owner-managers appeared daunted or intimidated by the word 'strategy'. A significant number have been involved in aspects of the strategy process without realising this, and many more have been put off by what they have read about so called 'corporate strategies'.

It is not difficult, however, to conduct a robust critique of this field of strategic management. Bantel and Osborne (1995) hold the twin "myths" of strategic management – generic, industry-specific strategy and the economies of scale – up to scrutiny and find them difficult to reconcile with the way in which dynamic businesses operate. The dynamic aspects of both internal business processes and innovations and the business environment have a profound effect on any identifiable link between performance and strategy.

The Problems of Contextualising Strategic Management in the SME Sector

The existing literature on strategic management, whilst being difficult to reconcile in terms of the conflicting theories outlined above, appears even further flawed in the SME context.

Attempts to derive an understanding of the strategic management process in SMEs has been constrained by a dominant debate. This is centered around short-term financial success and survival rather than long-term sustainability and 'strategic' aspects. Combine this with the entrepreneur's unwillingness or inability to model the dynamic processes of the internal interactions within the organisation or the interactions with its external environment and the problem becomes a more deep-rooted one. The idea that organisations can position themselves or strategically operate in 'good' and 'bad' industry structures or strategic groups is found to be flawed when attempted in the SME context. Coombs and Avrunin (1977) explore the relativity of 'good and bad' within the framework of dominating strategies and their insightful viewpoints may also be used to inform this debate. At a more fundamental level, 'good and bad' strategic planning or positioning may or may not lead to 'good or bad' strategic performance.

In recent years, much that has been sold into the SME sector under the guise of 'strategic' may even have had a detrimental effect. The way in which consultants, trainers and academics have aggrandised the mundane by placing the prefix 'strategic' before their offerings has resulted in the creation of an organisational and competitive comfort zone based on that which is operational, functional and above all, easy. In the SME sector the 'strategic question' remains difficult to resolve to the satisfaction of all parties.

Of even greater concern is the view that the prescriptive approach to the strategy process may lead to a search for a uni-linear route or single paradigm, justified by subjective or rational criteria. The unilinearity and simplicity of this approach, whilst attractive to many consultants, academics and practitioners, is problematic in that the dynamic complexity of the environment mitigates against it. The growth patterns and formalised strate-gic planning sold into SMEs as 'the business plan' is difficult to reconcile against the dynamics of environment, innovation and opportunity sensing explored later in this paper. Hamel (Reimann, 1994) identifies a unilinear view of corporate devel-opment by suggesting that there is now a typical 'corporate his-tory' described as "lurching from crisis to restructuring. Then re-engineering. Then, under enormous duress, they finally wind up searching for strategy regeneration". Prahalad and Hamel (1994) add that too much emphasis has been placed on imple-mentation and execution rather than conceptualisation in recent years.

The strategy process and much of the literature of strategic management is also problematic in that reification of the corpo-ration takes place. The strategic management process in the SME sector does not fall into this trap because of the close, often symbiotic interactions between the entrepreneur, the organisa-tion and the strategy being pursued. In many cases in the SME sector, strategies and strategic rhetoric are difficult to define or contextualise. What are often clearly identifiable, however, are the behaviours and actions of the owner-manager or entrepre-neur.

The lack of formalised planning and structure can also cause contextual problems in terms of case examples or the establish-ment of an existing body of literature in the strategy field. Yet this creates opportunities as well as problems. The strategic management process in SMEs is case-specific in that each context has a range of strategic variables and issues that may be widely diverse. Rather than SMEs not fitting the mould of the strategy process, strategic processes are difficult to reconcile with and transplant into the SME sector. There are a number of factors that mitigate against this process:

- Any vision of growth or configuration is emergent and rarely formalised by the entrepreneur.
- There is often a dichotomy between the business planning process (satisfying stakeholders) and the entrepreneur's long-term strategic view (often an informal or hidden agenda).
- The strategic paradigm is often not communicated to or agreed with other stakeholders by the entrepreneur.
- Strategies are emergent and adaptive.
- Strategic rhetoric is only used to communicate with peers and stakeholders. It is never used to communicate with employees. The strategic rhetoric and language of strategy and planning is often misapplied by those from the SME sector.
- The strategy process often lacks analytical credibility. There is often event contagion where the organisation is a hostage to fortune and events overtake and pollute any analytical clarity or reflection.
- The strategy process is often outcome or crisis-driven.
- There is often much choice and implementation without recourse to analysis, reflection and evaluation.

The difficulty of strategy-making in SMEs is often interrelated with problems of opportunity sensing. The wider the range of potential opportunities and the less risk-averse the entrepreneur or owner-manager, the greater the complexity and range of strategic variables which must be analysed. This in turn leads to a wider range of strategic responses, choices and potential strategies to be evaluated and implemented. In strategic terms, the flexibility of the SME is its greatest asset, but also a strategic 'Achilles heel' as the entrepreneur tries to realise a vast array of potential opportunities, often ending up with none or only one being translated into real strategies. This problem feeds back into the debate about unilinear and reductionist approaches to strategy-making discussed above. This issue is compounded by an unwillingness of owner-managers or entrepreneurs to involve themselves in the basic analytical and evaluatory processes that are fundamental requirements of the strategic management process.

If there is a single significant difference between the strategies of the SME and the large corporation, it is that they seem to be heading in different directions. Whilst SME strategies largely appear to be about growth and development, the corporate sector appears to have spent the last twenty years in a process of subdivision and shrinkage. The way in which SMEs grow and the strategies employed to promote and sustain growth are the real strategic issues in the SME sector and are what makes the SME sector the dynamic, innovative and visionary environment that it is.

The Fallacy of the Business Plan

Business planning and the production of a finished document – 'the business plan' – is one of the central tenets of the 'strategic' process in SMEs and business start-ups. Whilst it would be difficult to challenge the contextual orthodoxy of the business plan, there are too many case examples. It is useful to question entrepreneurs and owner-managers about why they feel that producing a business plan is a necessary element of the strategy process in the SME.

As Mintzberg (1994) points out, strategic planning is not strategy formulation. Formalised corporate planning often fails to reach the implementation phase; the planning process in practice often bears little resemblance to the strategy process.

The difficulty with the production of a business plan is that it is often grounded within a financial framework. The plan is usually produced to satisfy the information needs of a stakeholder, most notably the bank, and is often not referred to afterwards. What should be an enabling process often becomes a mere vehicle for justification, based solely on financial criteria and is ultimately a constraining factor. The variance between financially constrained business planning and a strategy perspective rests upon the issue of managerial choice. A more strategic perspective by default presents the owner-manager with more choice than purely financial criteria.

If used properly, the business plan is an enabling factor that allows the organisation to develop strategic responses to the issues it raises. It provides a supporting mechanism that underpins the process of convergence between the strategic intent(s) and objectives of the entrepreneur and the performance and resource realities of the business as an operational entity.

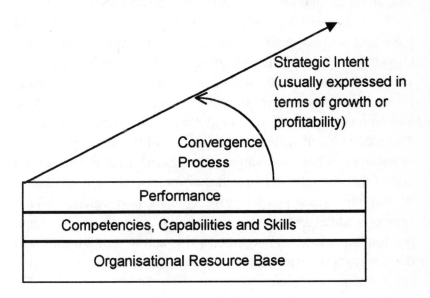

Structure and Scale versus Scope

The utilisation and appropriation of structure, be it environmental, industrial or organisational, is a key theme in the literature of strategic management. The structural aspects of competitive or industrial constructs underpin much of the traditional aspects of strategic analysis and strategic evaluation in the corporate and, by default, large organisational sector. This approach addresses the relativity of the organisation to its industry, although the size/structure debate here is problematic in that it favours large organisations that can leverage economies of scale. To merely assess the organisation's structure relative to the industry size and structure, however, over-simplifies the problem.

Within the SME sector, the narrow boundaries that identify the structural appear to be rapidly breaking down. Indeed, the rapid adaptation and adoption of new products, systems, structures, technologies and strategies by these SMEs prompts this author to pose the challenging view that, just as Stopford and Baden Fuller (1993) suggest, 'industry doesn't matter' and is increasingly being eroded in significance. This is occurring in that small businesses often define their scope, interpret their industry membership and configure their operations, systems and structures in order grow sustainable businesses.

If the dominant logic of the small firm sector is growth, then the question that must be asked is: "What type of growth?" Growth into physical space resulting in physically larger organisations with more storage and operational capacity is represented by the logic of economies of scale. This internalisation of space and structure is suited to a traditional, scale-oriented approach. The economies of scale argument is one of the fallacies of traditional approaches to strategic management as it is based on a notion that the size and structure of the organisation relative to its industry has a positive effect on its performance. This approach addresses the relativity of the organisation to its industry through debate centred around size and hegemony, although the size/structure/strategic success debate here is reductionist, simplistic and inadequate.

This is at variance with SMEs whose growth patterns can be identified by a quest for economies of scope. More recently, the scope of the organisation has been defined in terms of its reach, whether in geographical terms or in terms of product or service offerings. Other scope issues can be the range of people, information and resources that can be called upon. These potential economies of scope may take different forms, and this is reflected in terms of strategic stretch and leveraging internal resources in order to expand to exploit the potential opportunities

Unlike the IO model, it is no longer possible to make assumptions about the way in which scale and economies of scale affect the strategic and competitive process. Large, well-established, traditionally organised corporations still continue to exploit advantages based on scale. Organisational size in many markets and sectors is increasingly becoming a significant factor for strategic success.

By utilising a graphic representation of Clarke and Staunton's (1993) concept of the interactions of scale and scope, it is possible to identify the traditional route to growth pursued by SMEs as being thus:

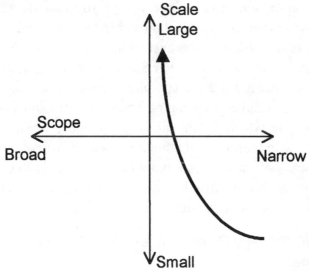

The way in which the structural aspects are correlated with scale is of interest to those studying the SME sector. Previously, business growth has been inextricably linked to scale. The growth patterns of SMEs have traditionally been forced through an isomorphic constraint that 'larger is better'.

Conformism and Isomorphism

The concept of the strategic group (Hunt, 1972) provides a real example of strategic isomorphism and crowding into perceived 'good' structural environments. The strategic group can be broadly defined as a group of firms producing goods or services that are close substitutes or imitations and broadly following the same set of strategies. The notion of the strategic group is essentially one that is steeped in IO theory.

The strategic group promotes competitive caution, conformism and isomorphism (Di Maggio & Powell, 1983) and it
may even inhibit innovation. Butler and Vit (1994) further suggest that the forces driving organisations towards isomorphism
include strategic planning methods that "enforce common procedures for thinking about the environment and the future", and
the need for organisations to respond to given performance
norms and the transfer of common norms through industry
groups and management associations. This conformist and isomorphic approach is described by Adorno and Horkheimer
(1972) as "a circle of manipulation and retroactive need in which
the unity of the system grows ever stronger".

At issue is the way in which SMEs have traditionally been
'grown' in order to fill the isomorphic expectations of stakeholders. This has resulted in planning norms and structures promot-
ed the way in which SMEs should grow and develop. When
combined with traditional IO thinking about industrial structure,
these isomorphic structures rapidly become a doubly constraining factor for commoditised, innovation-restricted and traditional organisations and industries.

The SME Strategy Process: Intent, Architecture and Resources

When considering the process of strategic management, the
application of what is considered to be strategic for the small
business is often much more limited by the scale and scope of
the business. The basics, however, are largely the same. There
are certain questions that owner-managers in SMEs should initially ask, as has been discussed in previous chapters. These are:

• Where are we now?

• Where do we intend to be?

• How will we get there?

These are not questions about future position alone, but questions of future direction for the business. The issue of time
frames is important in the SME sector due to the fact that what
may be long-term and strategic for an SME may be short-term

for a larger organisation. Strategic issues often become easy to identify over time, which suits the processes of strategy-making in SMEs.

The idea that there is a central strategic theme, a vision that drives the organisation and a process by which the organisation translates these factors into real strategies is an attractive one. There is scope for combining strategic intent with mission and vision (Campbell *et al.,* 1990) and planning and intent (Bates & Dillard, 1991). Many managers attempt to set strategy when operating in a realm determined by strategic intent and outside the bounds of their organisation's structures. This problem may be further compounded in the SME sector by the owner-manager's closeness to the enterprise.

Many owner-managers say they feel there is no clear link between their long term view of the business, the strategy that they communicate to their staff, the ideas that they communicate to lenders such as the bank and the realised action and implementation of these plans. Organisations that translate concepts, such as longer term vision and an innovative and distinctive view of their business, into real actions and outcomes are those that demonstrate enhanced levels of strategic awareness. Stopford and Baden Fuller (1994) suggest competitive battles can be based on each organisation's differing concept of corporate strategy. The idea that owner-managers need to embrace early on is that there *is* a central strategic theme or idea that drives them and their organisation, and a process by which they and the organisation translate these factors into real strategies.

This transition is processual and identifies and constructs an organisational future defined by Hamel and Prahalad (1994) as "strategic architecture". This is represented by a concept or vision of both the future competitive environment and 'strategic intent'. Owner-managers of SMEs should concentrate on the translation of this 'architecture' into profitable mainstream business activity. This is not as abstract as it initially seems in that oftentimes the owner-manager's strategic intent is emotionally linked to the product or service that they are involved with. Not only does the prod-

uct or service task represent the core competence of the organisation and provide links with the strategic intent, it also suggests a
hierarchy of priorities that place product and task first and identify
the systems, structures and cultures as supporting mechanisms.

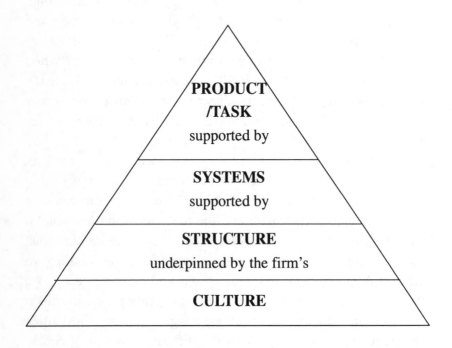

This model can be developed by suggesting that the firm's task
or product orientation represents its contact point with the wider
environment. The underpinnings of this are identified below.

Task

The task of the organisation is essentially what the organisation is
put together to perform. However, certain other tasks are often prioritised above the organisation's core task. In the SME sector, the
entrepreneur often focuses on this core task and utilises the skills
and resources available to develop competences and capabilities in
this area. The task is not, however, set in stone and there is an
ongoing need to redefine it. Problems can arise when other tasks
are introduced that are not linked with the core task.

Systems

In order to effectively support the task orientation of the organisation, certain operational systems can be put in place. Of primary concern is the development of systems that are 'out of control', and are set up to justify structural considerations. Additionally, other systems are put in place that do not support the activities or provide inadequate support.

Structure

Structure is (or should be) put in place to support the systems. Structure can be defined as the interaction between people within the organisation, their physical location and their hierarchical position within the organisation. Recently, however, the change from a role-based approach to a task approach to decision-making and problem-solving has resulted in less emphasis on the hierarchical aspects.

Culture

The culture of the organisation is a mix of factors that define the organisation both for those who work internally and the external stakeholders. It is the norms of behaviour and the day to day interaction that develops organically and naturally. Problems usually arise when culture is imposed.

It is now possible to identify the links between the elements of strategic intent, competitive advantage and notions of effectiveness and efficiency with the above model. These are underpinned by the competencies and resources identified above. However, in many SMEs these elements are often neglected or emergent.

The rationale for the above framework is that the entrepreneurial vision and strategic intent is that which defines the strategic context, and that everything flows directly from this source. The organisation is then concerned with striking a balance between concerns of internalised effectiveness and efficiency on the one hand and a quest for external competitive advantage on the other. The strategic context here represents a demarcation between internal and external objectives. These are limited in their contextualisation, but are identifiable as the early elements in a process of convergence between intent and reality. What shapes and defines this process are notions of adaptiveness, flexibility, uniqueness and strategic leadership, all of which are encompassed either by the entrepreneur's behaviours, competences and strategic intent or by elements of the task, systems structure and culture model.

The reconciliation of the behavioural aspects of the strategy process with the need for the analytical and evaluatory aspects is a key element of the materials developed for use with SME owner-managers. It is from this that it is possible to identify the following model, which seeks adaptation of these two aspects.

VISION
Opportunity sensing
Intuition
Mission

↓

STRATEGY
Analysis
Balancing plans/budgets (satisfy stakeholders)
Strategic choice
Strategic evaluation

Uniqueness: A Key Source of Competitive Advantage for the SME Sector

Quinn's (1980) definition of strategy as "a means for allocating resources into a *unique* and viable posture" serves as the starting point for this debate. If there is an optimum moment to consider unconventional or innovative approaches to the strategic management process, it may be now. There is an increasing body of literature (Reimann, 1994; Greer & Ireland, 1992) that highlights unconventional approaches to the functional activities commonly found in most organisations.

Harari (1994) suggests that effective strategy formulation and implementation relies on concepts of uniqueness and differentiation leading to sustainable competitive advantage, whereas traditional competitive analysis promotes conformism, caution and imitation of the key, often well-established major players in the industry.

Structural changes, excess capacity, environmental concerns, changed consumer priorities and technology and deregulation have all added to the need for radical and even unconventional rethinking of both the strategy process and the way in which strategy is communicated and disseminated.

The attention given to unconventional courses of strategic action might appear to be useful in the light of dynamic uncertainty in the environment: why go along with the crowd if no one is sure what is about to happen next? This was originally Schumpeterian's (1934) view, and has been updated by Prahalad and Hamel (1994), who suggest that managers are "abandoning traditional approaches to strategy".

Weick (1979) identifies the problems caused by organisational realities within the context of structured environments. Therefore, SME managers need to ask themselves what makes their business competitive, innovative and distinctive.

Since an unconventional approach is essentially theory-driven rather than problem-driven (for example, in the way that total quality management seeks to improve quality), a major problem is arriving at a definitive taxonomy of these approaches relevant to strategic management. Different approaches may be useful in different circumstances, and the author of this chapter would not seek to suggest that uniqueness or an unconventional approach can be wholly generic and transferable in the way that Porter's strategies are, for example, the strategy of cost leadership, which seeks to gain competitive advantage in the marketplace by offering the lowest cost products or services across a broad range of products or services. However, it is possible to identify the following general suggestions for developing a unique competitive advantage.

- Devise investment strategies based on future potential and competitive position rather than present demand.
- Question the dominant logic of the industry or strategic group.
- Question 'global' facts and figures in the light of 'local' knowledge.
- Develop autonomous approaches to strategy making.
- Nurture the ability to abandon unwritten rules and norms, particularly those that are 'imposed' or brought in from outside.
- Give managers and employees the authority to 'dismantle' the dominant logic that previously shaped the organisation.
- Search for different 'concepts' of strategy.
- Explore synergies between unconventional and conventional approaches.

It appears that much that might be considered unique or unconventional has been defined in terms of the research that looks at organisations displaying "unusual characteristics". Additionally, Hamel and Prahalad (1993) consider the creation of "new forms of competitive advantage", which might be further modified through the consideration of "different forms of competitive advantage". As Starbuck (1995) suggests, the competitive advantages of the future will come from the marginal, the unconventional, the accidental and the exception to the rule.

Whilst strategic management models are largely based on placing the variables of organisations, environments or the interaction of the two within easily recognisable boundaries, industry structures, frameworks or patterns of analysis, possibly of greater interest is the view that Levy (1994) suggests "there are usually far too many exceptions for the models to have much predictive effect".

Strategic Leadership and the Nature of Strategic Entrepreneurship

It would be remiss to end this chapter without making some reference to the leadership process and its integration with the strategy process in SMEs. The fact that strategies are entrepreneurially focused and often driven by charismatic leadership is supported by case research and the experiences of the team at Bolton Business School.

Entrepreneurial strategies are change-driven and reliant upon the development of new routines. By balancing the issues in the strategic management process, the owner-manager can achieve a close fit between what the organisation offers, its systems and structures and the wider environment. This model demonstrates the issues of fit between elements in the strategy process. It echoes aspects of Thompson's (1993) EVR Congruence Model in that it seeks to link both internal and external aspects of the strategy process.

```
                    ┌─────────────────┐
                    │    Strategy     │
                    ├─────────────────┤
                    │ Strategic Intent│
                    └─────────────────┘
            ┌─────────────────┐   ┌─────────────────┐
            │   Competitive   │   │  Organisational │
            │    Advantage    │   │   Effectiveness │
            │                 │   │   and Efficiency│
            └─────────────────┘   └─────────────────┘
                      ┌─────────────────┐
                      │      Task       │
                      ├─────────────────┤
                      │     Systems     │
                      └─────────────────┘
                      ┌─────────────────┐
                      │    Structure    │
                      └─────────────────┘
      ┌──────────────────────────────────────────────┐
      │              Functional Areas                │
      ├───────────┬──────────┬──────────┬────────────┤
      │ Operations│ Marketing│  Human   │  Finance   │
      │ Technology│          │Resources │            │
      │and Support│          │          │            │
      └───────────┴──────────┴──────────┴────────────┘
      ┌──────────────────────────────────────────────┐
      │               Cultural Factors               │
      └──────────────────────────────────────────────┘
```

By moving the organisation through the elements of this model without forgetting the original strategic intent, owner-managers can build an approach of sustained strategic competitive advantage whilst retaining a focus on matching capabilities and external requirements. This can be achieved in the longer term by supporting the product or service task with appropriate systems, structures and resources. The impetus for that process and for long-term sustained competitive advantage relies upon a concept of strategy and a mindset that can only be developed through strategic leadership from the owner-manager.

Conclusion

Entrepreneurial approaches to the strategy process are change-driven and reliant upon the development of new routines. It is proactive, experimental and relies on learning and breaking rules. The entrepreneur is by default unconventional and contra-distinctive. He or she often acquires the skills and knowledge of the entrepreneurial process in unformulated and unstructured ways.

As Burrell (1992) suggests, there may be alternative types of organisations with different structures that may be contra-distinctive alternatives to the bureaucratic hierarchy of traditional management thinking. This is borne out by the concept of a strategy/structure interface (Thompson, 1993) that identifies an implicit relationship between strategies and the 'shape' of organisations. It may be possible to draw a similar set of parallels by using the holistic Task, Systems, Structure, Culture model to shape the organisation's strategic architecture.

The difficulty with any organisation that appears to abandon the conformism and isomorphism of the modern enterprises is that it ceases to demonstrate the characteristics of what McNeil (1981) describes as "the modern industrial order". McNeil suggests that these characteristics are typified by the "fusion of the capitalist enterprise with a bureaucratic form of organisation". The Weberian construct of organisation as bureaucracy, whilst providing us with a polythetic species, also provides us with an example of conformism and isomorphism within the strategic group.

Rather than merely abandoning theoretical models of strategic management, it may be possible to develop multiple concepts of strategic 'managements', operating in multiple spaces with different contexts, architectures, strategic intents, realities and inputs and outputs. The SME context has and will continue to yield interesting theories, concepts and provocations, which will continue to refine and reform our notions of what is strategic and the strategy process.

It is to be hoped that this chapter is one of a series of provocations that will develop the ongoing debate about the way in which the strategic process is developing in innovative and unique ways in the SME sector.

References

Adorno, T W & M Horkheimer, *The Dialectics of Enlightenment* (London, first published in 1947) 1972, p. 121.

Aharoni, Y, "In Search of the Unique: Can Firm-Specific Advantages be Evaluated?" *Journal of Management Studies* (1993) Vol. 30, pp. 30-49.

Bantel, K A & R N Osborn, "The Influence of Performance, Environment and Size on the Identifiability of Firm Strategy" *British Journal of Management* (1995) Vol. 6, pp. 235-248.

Bates, D L & J E Dillard, "Desired Future Position – A Practical Tool for Strategic Planning" *Long Range Planning* (1991) Vol. 24, No. 3, pp. 90-99.

Brunsson N, *The Irrational Organisation* (Stockholm: Wiley) 1985.

Burrell G, "Back to the Future: Time and Organisation" in M Reed & M Hughes (eds), *Rethinking Organization* (London: Sage) 1992.

Butler, R & G Vit, "Contrarian Strategy: Perspectives Upon an Institutional Economy of Organisations" Working Paper 24.3 (Lancaster University: British Academy of Management Conference) September 1994.

Campbell, A, M Devine & D Young, *A Sense of Mission* (London: Century Business Press) 1990.

Caves, R E, "Industrial Organization, Corporate Strategy and Structure" *The Journal of Economic Literature* (March 1980) Vol. 28, pp. 64-92.

Clarke, P & N Staunton, *Innovation in Technology and Organisations* (London: Routledge) 1993.

Coombes, C, H & G S and Avrunin, "Single Peaked Functions and the Theory of Preference" *Psychological Review* (1977) Vol. 84, pp. 216-230.

Di Maggio, P J & W W Powell, "The Iron Cage Revisited: Institutional Isomorphism and Collective Rationality in Organizational Fields" *American Sociological Review* (1983) Vol. 48, pp. 147-160.

Greer, C R & T C Ireland, "Organizational and Financial Correlates of a 'Contrarian' Human Resource Investment Strategy" *The Academy of Management Journal* (1992) Vol. 35, No. 5, pp. 956-984.

Hamel, G & C K Prahalad, "Strategy as Stretch and Leverage" *Harvard Business Review* (1993) Vol. 71, No. 2, pp. 75-84.

Hamel, G, & C K Prahalad, *Competing for the Future* (Boston: Harvard Business School Press) 1994.

Harari, O, "Running in Circles" *Small Business Reports* (1994) Vol.19, No. 11, pp. 52-55.

Hunt, M S, "Competition in the Major Home Appliance Industry 1960-1970" (Harvard University: Unpublished PhD dissertation) 1972.

Katz, D & R Kahn, *The Social Psychology of Organizations* (New York: Wiley) 1966.

Levy, D, "Chaos Theory and Strategy: Theory Application, and Managerial Implications" *Strategic Management Journal* (1994, special edition) Vol. 15, pp. 167-178.

McKiernan, P & C Morris, "Strategic Planning and Financial Performance in UK SMEs" *British Journal of Management 5* (1994, special issue) pp. S31-S42.

McNeil, K, "Understanding Organisational Power: Building on the Weberian Legacy" in M Zey Ferrell & M Aiken (eds), *Complex Organisations: Critical Perspectives* (Glenview IL: Scott Foresman) 1981, pp. 46-48.

Mintzberg, H, "Strategy Making in Three Modes" *California Management Review* (1978) Vol. 16, No. 2, pp. 44-53.

Mintzberg, H, *The Rise and Fall of Strategic Planning* (New York: Prentice Hall) 1994.

Porter, M E, *Competitive Strategy: Techniques for Analysing Industries and Competitors* (New York: Free Press) 1980.

Prahalad, C K & R Bettis, "The Dominant Logic: A New Linkage Between Diversity and Performance" *Strategic Management Journal* (1986) Vol. 7, No. 6, pp. 485-501.

Prahalad, C K & G Hamel, "Strategy as a Field of Study: Why Search for a New Paradigm?" *Strategic Management Journal* (1994, special edition) Vol.15, pp. 5-16.

Quinn, J B, *Strategies for Change: Logical Incrementalism* (Homewood IL: Richard D Irwin) 1980.

Reimann, B C, "Gary Hamel: How to Compete for the Future" *Planning Review*, September/October 1994, pp. 39-43.

Shumpeter, J A, *The Theory of Economic Development* (Cambridge, MA: Harvard University Press) 1934.

Starbuck, W, *Keynote speech at the 1995 British Academy of Management Conference* (Sheffield University) 1995.

Stopford, J M & C Baden Fuller, *Rejuvenating the Mature Business* (London: Routledge) 1994.

Thompson, J L, *Strategic Managment – Awareness and Change* (London: Chapman and Hall) 1993.

Thurlow, B K, *The Nature of Belief* (Burlington VA: Fraser Publishing) 1990.

Weick, K, *The Social Psychology of Organization* (New York: Random House) 1979.